HOW TO SPEAK JEWISH

A mini-dictionary of Jewish words

(plus a lot of good stuff about what it means to be Jewish)

Joanie Chura

Copyright © 2007 by Joanie Chura

How To Speak Jewish
by Joanie Chura

Illustrations by Robert Chura

Printed in the United States of America

ISBN 978-1-60477-199-2

All rights reserved solely by the author. The author guarantees all contents are original and do not infringe upon the legal rights of any other person or work. No part of this book may be reproduced in any form without the permission of the author. The views expressed in this book are not necessarily those of the publisher.

Unless otherwise indicated, Bible quotations are taken from the New King James Version of the Bible. Copyright © 1982 by Thomas Nelson, Inc. Used by permission.

www.xulonpress.com

CONTENTS

INTRODUCTION:
  My Letter to the Reader   p. 5

PART ONE:
  Everyday Jewish Words   p. 13

PART TWO:
  The Jewish Holy Days   p. 75

PART THREE:
  Jewish Foods (with recipes)   p. 95

PART FOUR:
  The Language of Judaism   p. 117
  and Jewish Tradition

  (a) A Short (very short) History of the Jewish People

  (b) The 3 Branches of Judaism: Orthodox, Conservative and Reform

  (c) The 2 Main Jewish Groups: Ashkenazim and Sephardim

  (d) The Ancient Jewish Wedding

  (e) Common Words in Judaic Tradition

APPENDICES: p. 165

    The Jewish Mind-set
    The Jewish Life-Style
    Well-Known Jewish People

BIBLIOGRAPHY p. 187

Dear Reader,

I grew up in a Jewish neighborhood in Brooklyn and until I went to college I didn't know anybody who wasn't Jewish! When I did go to college all my Gentile friends were always after me to teach them Jewish words. My mother was dead set against this. She felt that anyone who used them would be labeled "coarse" and "uneducated." However, my friends were persistent and continued to wrench them out of me -- words like "klutz" and "shtick" and "schlep." And actually the more "educated" I became -- and I was educated up the kazoo -- the more I fell back on these words. Why? I guess because they expressed things which were impossible to express in English and, so far as I know, in any other language! They are also funny and fun to say because they are so onomato-poetica-retica. (The word is really "onomato-poetic", but Mel Brooks, one of those famous Jewish comedians, tacked on "a-retica" and I think it adds sizzle to the word so I just always say it that way.) Onomato-poetica-retica means that the word sounds like what it means -- like "schlep" sounds like dragging something, or "klutz" sounds like someone who trips over his own feet. And isn't this the way language is supposed to be anyway? I also began to see that as an extra added bonus Jewish words are a doorway to understanding what it means to be Jewish. So for all these reasons I decided to share them in this book.

Right off the bat I have to admit that I lied in the title. There is really no such thing as the Jewish language. What I am really talking about is Yiddish, and Yiddish itself is a real mish-mash (see "mish-mash," a terrific example of onomatopoetica-retica). What we know as Yiddish is basically a High Middle German (used in Germany from the 11th through the 15th centuries), with some differences in structure, spelling and pronunciation -- while borrowing words and phrases from Czech, Polish, Russian, French, Italian, and almost every other Slavic and Romance language. Its most prominent and well-known component is a considerable amount of Hebrew words and idioms. (Hebrew words are estimated to account for about 15-20% of Yiddish vocabulary.) There are also Yiddish words that were coined in America -- considered American-Yiddish slang, or "Americanish." (such as "schmo" and "schnook") Some institute tried to establish standard rules for spelling in 1937, but, according to Leo Rosten, these rules "have been rather widely ignored ever since."

So as for spelling, anything goes.

You might want to check out the appendices, one of which is "The Jewish Mind-set," or the Jewish belief system. It's always fascinating to see how what we think affects our behavior, even the way we walk and talk and dress and everything we do.

Anyhow, I hope you get a kick out of learning these Jewish (really Yiddish) words, and that they help you understand your Jewish friends. Oh, and I hope you get to laugh a little too!

Love,
Joanie

P.S. Leo Rosten's book, "The Joys of Yiddish," was an invaluable resource for me in writing my book. Thank you, Leo!

The Jews are just like everybody else --
only more so.
                    — Anonymous

    to this I would add:

The Jewish language is just like every
    other language -- only more so.

PART ONE

Everyday Jewish Words

baleboosteh

pronounced bal-eh-bust'-eh
Yiddish, a derivation of the masculine form, "baleboss" (bal-eh-booss') which comes from the Hebrew baal ha-bayet, "master of the house"

A baleboosteh is a fabulous homemaker -- someone who does everything -- cooking, cleaning, the laundry, etc., super-duper. (For example: "My mother was a real baleboosteh.") The trademark of a baleboosteh is that her house is so immaculate that you can eat off the floor (although I have yet to see anybody attempt this). There is somewhat of an obsession with cleanliness and hygiene among Jewish women -- at least that was the case when I was growing up. I have a feeling this harks back to previous centuries when, because of a lack of modern sanitation methods, cleanliness played an essential part in keeping the Jewish family healthy. It's probably in our DNA. Ver vase? (Who knows?)

13

bonditt

pronounced bon-ditt'
Yiddish, from the German bandit:
"rogue," "bandit"

A bonditt is a very mischievous child -- a very _very_ mischievous child. A bonditt is always looking for something "interesting" to do. When you leave a child alone in a room for a half hour and then when you check the room is totally "rearranged" (i.e. demolished), that child is a bonditt. Bonditts generally turn out all right because they are very clever and resourceful! They are really budding entrepreneurs. (Try telling that to the parents.)

bubeleh
 pronounced bub'-eh-leh
Yiddish, origin unknown, or possibly from the Russian/Slavic baba: "grandmother"

Bubeleh is a term of endearment, like darling or sweetheart. Jewish mothers call their children bubeleh all the time. (For example: "Come here bubeleh and I'll give you a hug.") The word oozes with love. You even have to purse the lips as if you are kissing someone when you say it. Leo Rosten says that mothers call their babies bubeleh because it carries the expectation that the child will one day be a grandparent. This is nice but a bit too schmaltzy for me. (see "schmaltz")

chotchke
pronounced chotch'-ka
Yiddish, origin unknown

A chotchke is a little something or other used for decoration which has no real purpose (except to clutter up the house!) As you can detect I'm not a chotchke fan, but in those cases where I'm forced to be around them I try not to look.

chozzerai

pronounced khoz-zair-eye' (the ch is a gutteral German kh -- beginning with a rattling in the back of the throat)
Yiddish, from the Hebrew chazir: "pig"

Chozzerai is anything awful, loathsome, even disgusting. (For example: "That movie was nothing but chozzerai.") Notice that this word derives from the Hebrew word for "pig." Jews don't like pigs. They're not kosher. (see "kosher")

chutzpa
  pronounced khoots'-pah
(the ch is a gutteral German kh––
beginning with a rattling in the back
of the throat)
Hebrew for nerve, "guts," gall,
      brazeness, boldness...

I could go on with more definitions, but nothing really captures the meaning of chutzpa because its equivalent does not exist in the English language. Among Jews it's considered a positive quality... sort of... I mean depending. On the good side it's gutsy, on the bad it's presumption or arrogance. (For example, good: "She had the chutzpa to jump up on the stage and give him a kiss!"; bad: "What chutzpa, to ask for more money!") Generally, we could all use a little more chutzpa... under certain conditions... depending.

farmisht
pronounced far-misht'
Yiddish, from the German mischen: "to mix"

Farmisht is used to describe someone who is confused or mixed-up. (For example: "Don't listen to her. She's all farmisht!") Farmisht refers to the mental realm, while "farpotchket" refers to being mixed up in the physical realm. (see "farpotchket") If you're ever around a bunch of intellectuals you will know what "farmisht" means.

farpotchket
pronounced far-potch'-ket
Yiddish, from the German patsche: "slap"

An adorable onomatopoetical-retical word. It means (and sounds) messed-up, sloppy, botched or bungled. (For example: "His internet site is so farpotchket!") The word is akin to farmisht (see "farmisht") except that farmisht is limited to the mental realm, whereas farpotchket refers to physical circumstances. Farpotchket is a very popular and versatile word in that it can describe anything from a book to a business.

Gevalt!
    pronounced ge-valt'
  Yiddish, from the German gewalt:
    "powers," "force"

Gevalt! when uttered by a Jewish person is definitely a cry to the Almighty for HELP! "Oy, Gevalt!" means, "Oh my God, look what happened! Help! A very popular word among Jews.

gelt
pronounced gelt (rhymes with felt)
Yiddish, from the German geld: "money"

We all know what gelt is. Gelt is actually worth more than American money (about 3¢ more per dollar on the foreign exchange.) (Don't believe me.)

gonif
pronounced gon'-iff
Yiddish, from the Hebrew ganov: "thief"

A gonif is a thief or scoundrel, a tricky, shady character. (For example: Don't take your eyes off him. He's a real gonif.") Leo Rosten says it can also mean a mischievous prankster or a rascal, but I never heard it used this way. In my circles a gonif was serious business with no redeeming social significance. The word "con-man" in English expresses the same thing. Most likely every language has a word for this universal type.

Gottenyu!
pronounced gawt'-en-yew
Yiddish, from the German Gott: "God"

Gottenyu! is an exclamation meaning "Dear God!", or "How-can-I-describe-my-feelings!" It is not meant to invoke God's help, as does "Gevalt!" (see "Gevalt!") but is used merely for emphasis by adding fervor. (For example: "Oy, Gottenyu!, was the house a mess!" or "Was I happy! Gottenyu!") Along with "Gevalt!" a very popular Jewish word.

goy, goyim (plural)
    pronounced goy (rhymes with boy)
  The plural is pronounced goy'-im
    Hebrew for "nation"

A goy is anyone who is not Jewish -- that is, a Gentile. The term can be purely descriptive, or sometimes (unfortunately) derrogatory -- due to the persecution of Jews by Gentiles over the centuries and the legacy of bitterness that resulted among many Jewish people.

shaygets (pronounced shay'-gits) is a Gentile man.
shiksa (pronounced shik'-seh) is a Gentile woman.
  both Yiddish, from the Hebrew shegues: "blemish"

Nowadays there is so much intermarriage between Jews and Gentiles that the words "goy" and "shaygets" and "shiksa" are generally neutral, descriptive terms. A good thing! (My goyisher husband would agree.)

haimish

pronounced haimish (rhymes with Danish)

Yiddish, from the German heim: "home"

Haimish means warm and cozy, but especially "informal," that is, unpretentious, down-to-earth. (The opposite of snobbish or uppity.) According to Leo Rosten a haimish person is someone with whom you can take your shoes off or let your hair down. The Jewish culture and Jewish people in general are definitely haimish.*

* see appendix, "The Jewish Mind-set"

Kibitzer

pronounced kib'-itz-er

From the German name for a bird, the Kiebitz, a lapwing, reputed to be especially nosy and inquisitive, and called colloquially, Kibitzer

In my circles a kibitzer was someone who jokes around a lot and teases. (For example: "He's such a kibitzer.") Both the dictionary and Leo Rosten says that it is also somebody who looks on (as in a card game) and gives unwanted and meddlesome advice. Sometimes it just means to have a talk or chat with someone -- something like "shooting the breeze." In that way kibitzing is akin to schmoozing (see "schmooze") but maybe with more laughs. I like to think of a kibitzer (according to the first definition) as a comedian in training -- and you can bet that they all think of themselves that way!

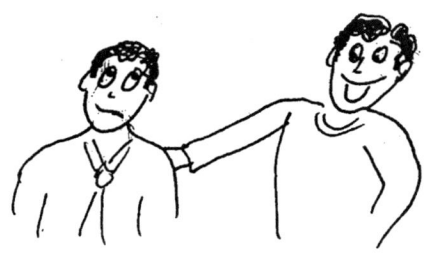

Kishka
pronounced kish'-ka
Russian for "intestines"

Kishka actually refers to a Jewish delicacy of meat, flour and spices, stuffed into intestine casing and baked. When I was a kid I lived for this--which generally was only to be had at Jewish weddings. Delicious is an understatement! But aside from food, kishka and kishkas also mean "guts" or "belly." (For example: "When she ignored me like that, it hit me in the kishka," or "I was laughing so much my kishkas were sore.") The Jewish mind-set doesn't know from a separation of body and soul.*

* see appendix, "The Jewish Mind-set"

Klutz

pronounced klutz (rhymes with mutts)
Yiddish, from the German klotz:
"wooden block"

As everybody knows a ktutz is somebody who is very clumsy, I mean very, very clumsy. (For example: Don't let him pick up that lamp. He's a klutz.") An indispensible word for which there is no English equivalent. Its usage is so common that we think of it as being English! A klutz can be very endearing, just so long as he doesn't spill that hot chicken soup on your lap.

Kosher

pronounced Ko'-sher
Yiddish, from the Hebrew Kasher:
"fit", "proper," "permissible"

Kosher actually means fit to eat because prepared according to the Jewish dietary laws. (There are also animals that the Bible does not consider to be food, and of course these animals are not "kosher" or permissible to be eaten.) But as we all know kosher has come to mean much more than that. Is there anyone, at least in America, who has not used "kosher" to indicate something that is proper, genuine, legitimate, etc. (For example: "Is this deal kosher?", or "Something is not kosher here", or "Are you sure it's kosher to give him that information?") The English language has been greatly enriched by this word, which has infiltrated every level of society, from presidents to plumbers. No other equivalent English word carries the same kind of authority as "kosher."

Kvell

pronounced Kvell (rhymes with swell)
Yiddish, from the German quellen:
"to gush," "to swell"

Kvell means to swell with immense pride and pleasure, usually over the achievements of a child. (For example: "You should have seen how she kvelled at her daughter's graduation.") In my circles it was also used to describe the rush of delight one feels at anything that makes one particularly happy. (For example: "Every time I look at my new bedroom set, I kvell.") It involves almost an audible "ahh." How Gentiles get along without this word I'll never know!

Kvetch

pronounced Kvetch ("rhymes with fetch") Leo Rosten says this word comes from the German quetschen: "to squeeze," "to press," and uses the example, "He manages to kvetch out a living." I never heard it used this way. In my circles it was strictly defined as a chronic complainer. (For example: "What is he kvetching about now?!")

We all know a kvetch and probably all of us have been one at some time or other. Jewish people do everything with excellence and they are particularly good kvetchers. You will know you are around a kvetch when you feel an irresistible urge to run the other way. Feel free!

macher

pronounced mokh'-er (the ch is a gutteral German kh -- beginning with a rattling in the back of the throat)

German for "maker," "do-er"

A macher is a big wheel, an "operator" -- someone who is active in organizing, fixing, arranging, someone with a lot of clout. (For example: "She's a big macher in the PTA.") Hint: Sometimes this is used in a negative sense, especially if the macher is arrogant or pushy. I guess the English equivalent is "leader", but macher says it better, don't you think? (It has more weight somehow.)

<u>machetayneste</u>
   pronounced mach-a-ten'-ista
(the ch is a gutteral German kh --
beginning with a rattling in the
back of the throat)
from the Hebrew mechutan,
   mechutenet: "relative (m. and f.)
         by marriage"

Machetayneste describes a relationship for which there is no word in English (and probably no other language). It is your daughter or son's mother-in-law. Where I come from it included the father-in-law as well. (For example: "My machetayneste is coming over for dinner." -- this meant that your son's or daughter's parents were coming over.) The fact that Jews give this relationship official status by naming it is an acknowledgement that not only does one have a new member of the family when a son or daughter marries, but that the two families are now united and that the parents of your new son or daughter-in-law are a ~~force~~ to be reckoned with!

There seems to be more machetayneste activity among Jews -- that is, more getting together of the two sets of in-laws. This is probably because when Jewish people marry the respective parents share the same cultural background and therefore have much in common. Nowadays there is so much intermarriage between Jews and Gentiles that a Jewish person's machetayneste could easily be Irish-Italian Roman Catholics. Oy, vey! (see "oy!")

<u>mavin</u>
>   pronounced may'-vin
>   Hebrew for "understanding"

A mavin is a connoisseur, an expert in something or other. (For example: "She's a real bagel mavin.") This term most often refers to a woman, which should tell you something.

mazel tov!
    pronounced ma'-zel tuff
    tov is Hebrew for "good"
    mazel is Hebrew for "luck"

Mazel tov! should not be taken literally to mean "good luck," but rather "congratulations!" or "Thank God!" You will hear mazel tov! resound at all Jewish celebrations -- births, graduations, and Bar Mitzvas, but especially at weddings, when, at the close of the ceremony, a glass wrapped in a napkin is placed on the floor and the bridegroom shatters it with his foot. At this point everyone shouts mazel tov! The breaking of the glass expresses sadness for the destruction of the Second Temple in Jerusalem and symbolizes the couples' break with their life before marriage, ushering in their new life together. (To be honest, the origin and meaning of this custom is a little speculative, but it sounds good, and anyway that glass is going to be broken no matter what. It wouldn't be a Jewish wedding without it, then the joyful shouts of mazel tov!, and the food, music and dancing that follow. If you've never been to a Jewish wedding you've never lived!)

mechaieh

pronounced ma-khy'-eh (the ch is a gutteral German kh -- beginning with a rattling in the back of the throat)
From the Hebrew chay: "life"

A mechaieh is something that gives great pleasure and joy -- from the littlest things to the greatest. When you take your shoes off at the end of a day and finally sit down, that's a mechaieh. When you see a beautiful painting or eat a wonderful meal, that's a mechaieh. Saying, "Oh, this is a mechaieh" is really expressing awareness of the gifts of God and gratitude for them. I think God likes that.

The Jewish toast, "L'chayim," offered before sipping wine at celebrations (pronounced La-khy'-im -- rhymes with fry 'em, with the same gutteral kh), means "to your health" and also comes from chay, the Hebrew word for "life." L'chayim literally means "to life."

megillah
   pronounced meh-gill'-eh
   (rhymes with guerilla)
   Hebrew for "scroll"

Megillah actually describes the scroll containing the Book of Esther in the Bible. This is read in the synagogue during the festival of Purim (see "Purim"). But it has come to mean anything that's overly long, complicated, detailed and boring. (For example: "Make it short and don't give me a whole megillah.") Women have a tendency to go into a whole megillah more than men, but women are prettier.

<u>mensh</u>

    pronounced mensh (rhymes with bench) from the German mensch: "person"

Among Jewish people the finest thing you can say about a man is that he is a mensh. (For example: "Now there is a real mensh.") This is another one of those no-equivalent-in-the-English-Language-words. A mensh is a person who has integrity -- someone who is honorable, decent and reliable, someone worthy of the utmost respect. This has nothing to do with whether the person is successful or wealthy. It is based solely on character. A rich man can be a schlemiél (see "schlemiél"), a doctor can be a schnook (see "schook"), but a poor or uneducated man can still be a mensh. Strangely enough, I have never heard a woman being called a mensh. Maybe it's because the word "man" is part of the spelling. I have to think about this.

meshugge
    pronounced mesh-shug'-geh
      Hebrew for "crazy"

meshugena
    pronounced mesh-shug'-gena
      Hebrew for "a crazy person"

(For example: You can either say, "He's a little meshugge," or "He's a real meshugena.")

Meshugge and meshugena are generally used in a humorous sense to describe a person who's a little wacky, eccentric or silly. A better example of onomatopoetica-retica would be hard to find! Kooks are definitely a little meshugge, but I have been one my whole life and I wouldn't give it up for anything. My motto is, if you have one life to live, live it as a kook. (even though some might call you a meshugena)

mishegoss
    pronounced mish-eh-goss'
      Hebrew for craziness

Mishegoss is used to describe a situation, idea, fad, etc. that's a little off the wall. (For example: "I don't believe the mishegoss that goes on in that house!" "Have you heard about the latest mishegoss she's into?!")

Warning: These words are used very often by Jews who over the centuries have cultivated a strong sense of the absurd. Where would the world be without Jewish comedians? (Comedy runs in our veins.) As to why this is, I think it relates to all the pain and suffering the Jewish people have endured throughout the centuries. Let me explain: Most jokes, comic situations, etc. come out of pain viewed in retrospect -- that is, at the time the situation took place it was far from funny -- in fact it was painful! Laughter is a way of releasing the pain (modern psychology would probably use the term "processing the pain"), thereby getting rid of anger and bitterness. (You can't be angry and bitter and laugh at the same time.) Laughter is then chicken soup for the soul. Anyway, that's *my* theory as to why there are so many Jewish comedians (because comedy is birthed in pain). I know you didn't expect to find something like this in a dictionary of Jewish words but I threw it in at no extra cost.

mish-mash
    pronounced mish-mosh
        (mosh rhymes with nosh)
  Yiddish, from the German mischen:
         "to mix"

As most of you already know, a mish-mash is a collection of unrelated things, a hodge-podge or jumble. It also means a confused or disordered mess. (For example: "That book is a real mish-mash of ideas," or "There is such a mish-mash of things in that store!") A better example of onomatopoetica-retica you won't find!

mishpochah

pronounced mish-pookh'-ah
(the ch is a gutteral German kh --
beginning with a rattling in the back
of the throat)

Hebrew for "family"

Mishpochah can sort of be defined as extended family. (For example: "My mishpochah is coming over for the holidays.") but this really doesn't do it justice. There _is_ the idea that it includes all the relatives -- both far and near. <u>But most Jews think of all other Jews as mishpochah.</u> (An astounding concept and the secret to the closeness of the Jewish community! *) Jews have a way of adopting outsiders or strangers (non-Jews) into the family, thereby automatically making them mishpochah. It's a long-standing Jewish cultural tradition going all the way back to the Book of Leviticus in the Bible in which God commands: "The stranger who dwells among you shall be to you as one born among you, and you shall love him as yourself; for you were strangers in the land of Egypt." (Leviticus 19:34) Count yourself to be extremely blessed to be adopted and part of the mishpochah -- everybody should belong to a nice Jewish family! It's like taking a warm bath in kosher milk.

* see appendix, "The Jewish Mind-set"
   A little personal anecdote to illustrate this:

When my Jewish grandmother, who came to America from Russia in the early part of the last century, would hear about someone involved in an accident in the neighborhood she would always ask, "Was he Jewish?" If the answer was yes, there would be a mournful "Oy, vey!" (see "oy!"). She was feeling for the person as if he were a member of her own family. I'm not saying that this is so commendable in that she didn't feel the same way about non-Jews who got into accidents. But it is remarkable that this uneducated Jewish woman (I'm not even sure if she could read) felt herself to be part of an extended family -- the whole of the Jewish community -- that included millions of people!

Yiddish names for the mishpochah:
   (family members)

father	tata (tah'-teh) or papa
mother	mame (mah'-meh)
husband	mann (mon)
wife	froy (rhymes with toy)
son	zun (zuhn)
daughter	tochter (tawkh'-ter)
brother	bruder (broo'-der)
sister	shvester (shves'-ter)
uncle	onkel (awn'-kel)
aunt	tante (tahn'-teh)
grandchild	aynkel (ane'-ek-el)
grandfather	zayde (zay'-deh)
grandmother	bubbe (bub'-beh)
father-in-law	shver (shvayr)
mother-in-law	shviger (shvi'-ger)

<u>mitzvah</u>
   pronounced mitz'-veh
   Hebrew for "commandment"

Mitzvah is a commandment of God, of which there are said to be 613! 248 are positive (such as caring for widows and orphans) and 365 are negative (such as not accepting a bribe).

Mitzvah also means the fulfillment of a commandment -- a truly good, kind, ethical deed. Jews are always performing mitzvoth (plural). It is important that they are not done from a sense of duty, but out of desire and with a joyous heart. If you do something really nice, a Jewish person may proclaim: "Oh, that was a mitzvah!"

mutche
pronounced mutch'-eh
Yiddish, from the Russian mutchit:
"to torture," "to torment"

To mutche somebody is to nag them to death -- "torture" and "torment" says it all. (For example: "Stop mutchering me, I'll do it tomorrow!") Every child at some point feels unmercilously mutchered by his or her parent. Especially teenagers.

naches
pronounced nach'-ess (the ch is a gutteral German kh -- beginning with a rattling in the back of the throat)
Yiddish, from the Hebrew nachatt:
"contentment"

One of those no-equivalent-in-the-English-language-words, naches is a combination of pride, pleasure and joy, the glow that comes from the achievements of a child. (For example: "My son the doctor gives me such naches.") Naches sounds so much more substantial than pride, doesn't it. You can almost taste it. Not only that, but when you get a lot of naches it makes you kvell. (see "kvell")

<u>nebech</u> or <u>nebbish</u>
   pronounced neb'-ekh (the ch is a guttural German kh -- beginning with a rattling in the back of the throat)
   also pronounced neb'-ish
     Yiddish, origin unknown

Nebech is the Yiddish equivalent for the English "nerd". But whereas nerd sounds a bit cold and unfeeling, nebech definitely carries a note of pity and compassion. (For example: "That poor nebech lost his job again.") This is true of even the most uncomplimentary Yiddish words. (It's a well known fact that chicken soup softens the heart.)

nosh
    pronounced nosh (rhymes with gosh)
    Yiddish, from the German nashchen
    "to nibble"

A nosh is anything eaten between meals. (For example: "Have a little nosh before dinner.") This is one of those words that have become so common that we think of it as being English. A nosh is more delicious than a snack but more fattening.

nu

pronounced nu (rhymes with shoe)
Russian for "well", or "well now"

Nu means "Well?" or "So what happened?" (For example: "I saw you coming out of her house. Nu?" another example: "Nu, did he marry her?")

It can also mean, "What are you waiting for?" (For example: "You're supposed to be at the dentist in 5 minutes. Nu?")

It can also mean, "How are things with you? or "What's new?" (For example: "Nu?")

If you are Jewish, nu is one of those indispensible, but barely definable words. (also, see "oy!") "Nu?" was first coined by Moses when he was waiting for the Israelites to cross over the Red Sea. (I'm being silly.)

nudnick

pronounced nud'-nick
Yiddish, origin unknown or possibly from the Polish nudny: "tiresome" and nuda: "boredom"
a nudnick is a pest, a nag

A nudnick is someone who is worthy of an Olympic (or should I say Oy-Lympic) Medal in pestiness, a relentless and intolerable nag, nag, nag. Both the dictionary and Leo Rosten say it also means a bore, but I never heard it used this way. Where I come from it was most often used to describe a particularly annoying small child. Every mother knows what a nudnick is!

<u>ongepotchket</u>
    pronounced ong'-qe-potch-ket
    Yiddish, from the Russian pachkat:
    "to soil", "to sully"

Ongepotchket sounds exactly like what it means -- overdone, overly decorated, much too much. (For example: "Oy, her house is so ongepotchket!")

I love this joke:

Sam strikes it rich and hires a famous abstract artist to paint a mural in his new house. He hangs a curtain to conceal it and has his friends over for the unveiling. When the curtain is pulled back there is one black dot in the middle of the wall. Everyone applauds. Sam goes over to his friend Herbie and asks him how he likes the mural. Herbie says its OK, but he wants everybody over to his house next week to unveil his own mural. The next week they all arrive at Herbie's house, the curtain is pulled back, and there are 2 black dots in the middle of the wall. Herbie goes over to his friend Sam and asks, "Well, how do you like it?" Sam answers, "Nice, but a little ongepotchket."

My case rests.

oy!

pronounced oy!
Yiddish, origin unknown

If you don't know what oy! means, oy!, what can I say? "Oh no" doesn't do it justice. "Oy!" just comes out of Jewish people naturally, like sneezing. (For example: "Oy!, he's coming over in 2 minutes and I'm not dressed yet!") "Oy-oy!" is more emphatic. (For example: "Oy-oy!, I see him pulling into the driveway!") "Oy vey!" (more emphatic still) is a shortened version of "oy vey iz mir!" (pronounced oy vay' iz meer), which literally means "oh woe is me." (Vay comes from the German weh, meaning "woe".) (For example: "Oy vey!, he got out of his car and his mother is with him!") I can't even imagine living without this word. It would be like being mute. If you're around someone who claims to be Jewish who never uses "oy!", don't believe him.

plotz
pronounced plotz (rhymes with tots)
Yiddish, from the German platzen:
"to burst"

Plotz means to split or burst or explode, but it is one of those all-purpose words which can be used in loads of different contexts. You can plotz from being happy or joyful. (For example: "Stop making me laugh or I'll plotz!") You can also plotz from aggravation, as in "He makes me so mad I could plotz!" No Jewish person ever goes very long without coming dangerously close to plotzing. It's part of our (very emotional) heritage.

potchkee
pronounced potch'-ka or potch'-kee
Yiddish, from the German patsch: a "slap"

The word "potch" is a slap, but potchkee means something entirely different. It means to "mess around" inefficiently. (For example: "I potchkeed around in the kitchen all day long," or "She potchkees around in the garden and calls herself a gardener.") Everybody has an area in which they have a tendency to potchkee. It's probably therapeutic.

schlemiel
pronounced schleh-meal'
Yiddish, origin unknown
Some say this word comes from a Shelumiel in the Bible, the son of the leader of the tribe of Simeon in Numbers 2. I see no evidence for this, as the Bible never mentions Shelumiel as being schlemiel-like (see below). Maybe this comes from Jewish oral tradition, but I doubt it. I just think the words happen to be similar.

schlimazel
pronounced schleh-maz'-el
from the German schlimm: "bad" and the Hebrew mazel: "luck"

schmo
pronounced schmo (rhymes with know)
Americanish (American-Yiddish slang)

schnook
pronounced schnook (rhymes with took)
Americanish (American-Yiddish slang)

shmegegge
pronounced shmeh-geg'-ee
Americanish (American-Yiddish slang)

<u>shmendrick</u>
    pronounced shmen´-drick
According to Leo Rosten, from the name of a character in an operetta by Abraham Goldfaden.

All these words mean essentially the same thing, with some controversy about the distinctions between them (which I won't get into because you could go crazy from that.) Does anyone in America <u>not</u> know that schlemiel, schlimazel, schmo, schook, shmegegge and shmendrick describe a person who is consistently a loser, someone for whom nothing seems to turn out right. They can also refer to a clumsy, all-thumbs type, a chronic bungler, someone who is maybe a little stupid or foolish. (A schmo particularly is someone who is stupid.) All of these words definitely carry a note of compassion. Anyone so described is more to be pitied than despised. ("For example: What did that poor schlemiel do now?")

As to why there are so many Yiddish words for this type is a good question. My theory is that when a people undergoes an incredible amount of suffering and persecution (like the Jews) it either produces someone with a victim mentality or someone who rises to the challenge and is an overcomer, a great achiever. We all know about the achievements of the

Jewish people. I read somewhere that 20% of Nobel Prize winners were Jewish (Jews comprise only 1/10th of 1% of the world population), and about 1/4 of all professionals in the U.S. are Jewish. (This is in a country where Jews are 2% of the population.) I can't remember where I read this. You'll just have to believe me. (So much for scholarly research.) Apparently the Jewish experience also produced its share of people who took the other route and consider themselves perpetual victims -- schlemiels, schlimazels, etc. There doesn't seem to be as many schlemiels as there used to be however, which is a good thing except that (alas!) one doesn't get as much of a chance to use these great onomatopoetica-retical words!

schlep

   pronounced schlep (rhymes with pep)
Yiddish, from the German schleppen:
   "to drag"

Schlep is a very versitile word.

As everybody knows, to schlep means to drag a lot of stuff from one place to another with weariness or difficulty. (For example: "I don't feel like schlepping all those clothes to the yard sale.")

It can also refer to a long, uncomfortable trip. (as in, "It was a real schlep to go from Chicago to Philadelphia.")

It can also mean to plod around laboriously (as in, "He schlepped around town all day looking for wallpaper.")

It can also mean a kind of clumsy or stupid person. ("He's such a schlep!")

Did I tell you, a very versitile word!

schlock
pronounced schlock (rhymes with mock)
Yiddish, origin unknown

Schlock is a cheap, poorly made piece of merchandise. (For example: "That's a real piece of schlock!") A schlock-house is a store that sells such merchandise. Jewish people avoid schlock like the plague. We try to buy only the best (wholesale if possible!) because it lasts longer and besides it's nicer.

schmaltz
pronounced schmaltz
Yiddish, from the German schmalz: "fat", "drippings"

Aside from its other meanings, schmaltz is actually melted fat -- usually chicken fat, which is very delicious spread on bread. (You won't find this in a health food store.) Schmaltz has come to mean anything overly sentimental, "corny," or "mushy," "dripping" with sugary sweetness. (For example: He always sings these schmaltzy songs.") I myself have very little tolerance for schmaltz. When people are taking out their hankerchiefs, I'm running for the door. (I have to. My schmaltz detector goes off.)

schmatte

pronounced schmatt'-ah (rhymes with lot-a)

from the Polish szmata: a "rag," "piece of cloth"

A schmatte is an old cloth or rag. It is used to describe some piece of fabric that has seen its last days. (For example: "Did you see that old schmatte she put on the bed?!" or "That dress looks like a real schmatte!") The clothing industry is referred to as the schmatte trade. I had an uncle who used to call a weeping willow a schmatte tree. (A brilliant observation.)

<u>schmeer</u>
   pronounced schmeer (rhymes with hear)
Yiddish, from the German schmiere:
   "grease" or "bribe"

A schmeer is a bribe. It has long been a part of American-Yiddish slang and is related to "greasing the palm." (For example: "Do you think he'll take a schmeer?") It also means "the whole deal", or "the whole package." (For example: "He bought the whole schmeer, from the kitchen chairs to the bedroom set," or "When he dressed up as Santa Claus he put on the red suit, the boots, the beard, the whole schmeer.") In answer to the obvious question as to what the first definition has to do with the second, the answer is, I have no idea. It's just one of those things.

schmooze

pronounced schmooze (rhymes with ooze)
Yiddish, from the Hebrew shmuos:
"things heard," "rumors," "idle talk"

To schmooze means to have a warm friendly chit-chat -- a _prolonged_ warm friendly chit-chat. (For example: "They're schmoozing on the back porch.") Schmoozing is more cozy and affectionate than talking. 8 out of 10 psychiatrists say schmoozing is absolutely essential for mental health. (I made that up.)

schnorrer
    pronounced schnor'-rer
    (rhymes with snorer)
  Yiddish, from the German schnorren:
    "to beg"

A schnorrer is the Yiddish equivalent of a moocher, according to Leo Rosten, but to be honest I never heard it used this way. Where I come from it described a real cheapskate and bargain hunter, someone who was known to hoard money. (For example: "That schnorrer didn't even leave a tip.") Schnorrers are not fun to be around. They lack faith in the provision of God. (I never thought of it that way before, but it's true.)

shipatsibeleh
    pronounced ship-a-tsib'-e-leh
  Yiddish, origin unknown

This is the only word I couldn't find anywhere, but my mother taught it to me and mothers don't lie. My only clue is that the word "tsibeleh" in Yiddish means "onion", and an onion is little and thin and green (new).

A shipatsibeleh is a preemie, a baby born in the 7th month of pregnancy. This is a very cute word, just perfect to describe a cute little teeny weeny.... shipatsibeleh.

shm – not a word, but a prefix, which when added to a word pooh-poohs it -- Jewish people seemed to have invented this construction.

For example:
"The doctor says she has a virus. Virus-shmirus, she'll be better tomorrow."

"He has a daughter. Daughter-shmaughter, does she ever come to see him?"

"Counselor-shmounselor, he can't even talk to his own wife."

The suffix – nik, is also a Jewish invention, which when added to a word makes it a label for an enthusiastic practitioner of something. Some examples: beatnik, no-goodnik, neak nik

Both very creative linguistic devices, in mine humble opinion, among loads of others such as answering a question with a question. Example:
Q: "Will you marry me?"
A: "Will I marry you?"
    (meaning, "of course!")

There are also the wonderful "Who knew?" and "Go know!" as in "Who knew? or go know! I would write such a crazy book!"

shmutz
pronounced shmutz (rhymes with puts)
Yiddish

Shmutz is dirt and shmutzik means dirty. I ask you, doesn't "shmutz" sound much dirtier than "dirt". That's why I love Yiddish words.

shtarke
pronounced shtarke'-ah
Yiddish, from the German stärke: "strength"

A shtarke refers to someone who is very strong, and where I come from it is almost always used to describe a woman who has the strength of a man. (For example: "She loaded that truck all by herself. She's a real shtarke.") A shtarke is built a little more solidly too, as you would imagine. I am not a shtarke, but I wish I was sometimes. Sometimes not.

shtik
pronounced shtik (rhymes with pick)
Yiddish, from the German stück: "piece"

Shtik has infiltrated its way into the English language and most Americans know roughly what it means. I say "roughly" because it is one of those words that are hard to define. It's kind of a piece of "business" or clowning. (For example: "When he started going into his shtik we all burst out laughing.") In theatrical circles it can refer to a device (such as a gesture or facial expression) meant to steal attention, as in, "That actor uses the same shtik over and over." A lot of comedians are famous for a particular shtik (such as Groucho Marx raising his eyebrows and flicking his cigar). It has also come to mean anything that one does over and over (maybe a little compulsively), as in, "Every night she goes into her shtick of rearranging the furniture." I guess all of us have a shtick or two. (My husband has 17.)

tsimmes

pronounced tsim'-mess
from two German words --
zum: "to the" and essen: "eating"

Tsimmes is actually a stew of vegetable and/or fruits, cooked slowly over very low heat. Since tsimmes had so many ingredients and took such a long time to make, the word has come to refer to an involved complicated mess, a mix-up, a real stew. (For example: "She created such a tsimmes!") When you say, "Don't make such a big tsimmes out of it", you are saying, "Don't blow it up out of all proportion, don't make it such a big deal." (Mother-in-laws are experts when it comes to making a big tsimmes.)

<u>tsuris</u>
   pronounced tsaw'-riss
  Yiddish, from the Hebrew tsarah:
     "trouble"

Tsuris means trouble and/or aggrravation. (For example: "His son is giving him so much tsuris!" "Eat that broccoli and don't give me any tsuris!") As you can see from the examples, children are a prime source of tsuris, but on the other hand, are also a prime source of naches. (see "naches") It seems as if you want naches, you've got to go through a little tsuris so in the end you can kvell. (see "kvell") Am I going too fast?

tuchis or tush

tuchis is pronounced tukh'-is (the ch is a gutteral German kh -- beginning with a rattling in the back of the throat)
Hebrew for "under," "beneath"
tush is pronounced tush (rhymes with push)
Yiddish, probably a shortened version of tuchis

Tuchis or tush means the rear end or the buttocks. These words have become so commonly used that many people think that tush, at least, is English. "Get off your tuchis," or "Get off your tush", means "Get going already, move!" "A potch in tuchis" is a spanking or a slap on the behind. ("Potch" means a slap or a smack in Yiddish.) Where I come from "tushy" was also widely used. (A very cute word, especially descriptive of a baby's rear end.)

yenta

    pronounced yen'-ta
    Yiddish, origin unknown
    a gossip, a busybody

A yenta is a woman -- I never heard a man referred to as a yenta -- who has to know everything and tell everything, someone who pries into the affairs of others without mercy. (For example: "She's such a yenta!") There are Jewish women -- and I'm sure those of other ethnic persuasions -- who have elevated this to an art form.

zaftig
    pronounced zaff'-tig
  Yiddish, from the German saftig: "juicy"

Zaftig is the Yiddish equivalent for "built" in English. (speaking of a woman) Enough said.

zetz
    pronounced zetz (rhymes with pets)
  Yiddish, from the German setzung, literally "a setting back"

A zetz is a strong punch or a blow. (For example: "He gave me such a zetz!") Sometimes its not so strong but just playful or maybe a warning. (For example: "When her husband started telling that story, she gave him a zetz.") Zetzes speak louder than words.

zhlub

pronounced zhlub (rhymes with rub)
Yiddish, from the Slavic zhlob:
"coarse fellow"

A distinctly onomatopoetical-retical word. A zhlub is a clumsy oaf. It also can refer to someone who's just plain coarse -- insensitive and ill-mannered. (For example: "Did you see how that zhlub acted at the wedding!") A zhlub is not as endearing as a klutz (see "klutz") because klutziness is a physical thing, whereas zhlubiness extends to the whole person.

PART TWO

The Jewish Holy Days

Sabbath
    pronounced Sabb´-ath (English)
in Hebrew Sabbath is Shabbat,
    meaning "rest" or "cessation of labor,"
      pronounced Sha-batt´
in Yiddish Sabbath is Shabbes,
      pronounced Shah´-biss

The Lord says in the Book of Exodus in the Bible: "Work shall be done for six days, but the seventh is the Sabbath of rest, holy to the Lord....It is a sign between me and the children of Israel forever; for in six days the Lord made the heavens and the earth, and on the seventh day He rested and was refreshed." (Exodus 31:15,17) The Sabbath is a gift of rest and refreshment given by the Lord to His people. It is an incredible institution in which one day of the week is dedicated and devoted entirely to God. It begins just before sunset on Friday when the wife, dressed in her very best, lights the Shabbes candles, closes her eyes, and blesses God and prays for her family. The father then returns from services at the synagogue to bless his children and welcome the Sabbath, "the Queen of the week." The traditional Shabbes feast is then eaten. It usually includes gefilte fish (see "gefilte fish"), matzo-ball soup (see "matzo"), challah (see "challah"), roast chicken and tzimmes (see "tzimmes") and other things like chopped liver, apple sauce, etc. On Saturday there is the traditional lunch, prepared on Friday afternoon, since no work was to be done on that day. (The day for Jewish people begins at sunset and ends at the next sunset.) Lunch is usually cholent (a big stew) and kugel (see "Kugel").

On the Sabbath (Friday night to Saturday night) the Jews pray, study, discuss the Torah and Talmud (see "Torah" and "Talmud") and fathers and grandfathers engage their children in discussions of God's commandments, religious concepts and ethical problems. Leo Rosten has an interesting commentary on this: "I leave it to cultural historians to appraise the magnitude of the consequences of an entire people, young and old, spending one day a week, year after year, generation after generation, century after century, in a seminar on religion, morals, ethics, responsibility."

It is a custom for Jews to invite a stranger, a traveler, a student or a poor man, to share the Shabbes meal. Jews regard hospitality as an outstanding mitzvah or worthy deed (see "mitzvah"). Leo Rosten remarks: "It is hard to over estimate how this served to make Jews everywhere feel part of one universal fellowship. (see "mishpochah")

Shabbes ends at sundown on Saturday with a service called Havdala (chahv-dol'-lah), marking the separation of the Sabbath from the rest of the week. (In Hebrew havdala means "separation.") A special braided candle is lit, wine is poured and blessings are spoken.

The following is a wonderful description of the Sabbath by Harry Golden as he remembers life on New York's Lower East Side in the early part of the last century. (It is quoted in Leo Rosten's book, "The Joys of Yiddish"):

> "The Irish and Italian boys had Christmas once a year; we had exaltation every Friday. In the most populous neighborhood in the world, rent by the shouts of peddlers, the screams of children, and the myriad noises of the city, there was every Friday evening a wondrous stillness, an eloquent silence. So quiet was it that two blocks from the synagogue you could hear the muffled chant of the cantor and the murmured prayers of the congregation. Once the service was over, you came home to find your mother dressed in her wedding dress with a white silk scarf around her head. And your father told you all the sufferings

throughout the centuries were dedicated for this moment, the celebration of the Sabbath."*

In Jerusalem today, the Orthodox Jewish Quarter is blocked to traffic as soon as the Sabbath approaches, and there is that same "wondrous stillness."

The commemoration of the Sabbath has distinguished the Jews from the rest of the world as a people separated unto God. The Sabbath maintained their continual contact with the Divine. A famous observation says: "More than the Jews have kept the Sabbath, the Sabbath has kept the Jews."

---

* Leo Rosten got this quote from: Hutchins Hapgood, "The Spirit of the Ghetto," Funk and Wagnalls, 1966, p. 26

Passover

   pronounced Pass'-over
also called Pesach, pronounced Pay'-soch
(the ch is a gutteral German kh -- beginning
with a rattling in the back of the throat)
   Pesach is Hebrew for "to pass over," "to spare"
also known as "The Feast of Redemption"
  (see the Book of Leviticus in the Bible: 23:5,6)
      observed in March/April

Passover is a celebration of God's miraculous deliverance of the Israelites from enslavement in Egypt as recorded in the Book of Exodus in the Bible.** It is called "Passover" because God instructed his people to sacrifice a lamb and place the blood on the doorposts of their homes. Any home that had the blood of the Passover lamb was "passed over" on that night of the plague of death. Every first-born Egyptian died, while the Israelites were spared and set free the following day. So important is Passover to the present-day Jewish people that every Jew is required to think of himself as being personally delivered from Egyptian bondage by the God of Israel.

Passover is really a one day holiday, but it is combined with the 7-day Feast of Unleavened Bread (see "matzo"). The entire 8 days are commonly celebrated together as Passover. On the first or second night there is a ceremonial meal with liturgy called the Seder (pronounced say'-der). A Seder is an experience! It is a full-fledged meal as well as a service which includes loads of participation, music and fun. Most of all it is a celebration is the form of a living drama in which God uses seeing, hearing, touching, smelling and tasting to teach His Truth. If you get a chance to go to a Seder you will get a real feel for what it means to be Jewish.*

* see appendix, "The Jewish Mind-set"

** see: "A short (very short) history of the Jewish people"

Shavuot or Shavous
   pronounced shah-voo'-oat or
            shah-voo'-ose
   Hebrew for "weeks"
(see the Book of Leviticus in the Bible: 23: 15-21)
      observed in May/June

Shavuot is also known as "The Feast of Weeks" because it comes 7 weeks after Passover. It is also referred to as "Pentecost" because it falls 50 days after Passover. (pente = 5) This is a celebration of the spring harvest in which the Israelites were to rejoice over the ingathering of the wheat crops. Jewish tradition says that God gave the Torah to Moses on this day. (see "Torah") Some people celebrate by reading the Torah all night and eating dairy products, especially delicacies made of cheese, like cheesecakes and cheese blintzes. (see "blintzes") Why dairy products I don't know, but it sounds like a good idea to me, especially the blintzes part. Who am I to argue with TRADITION!

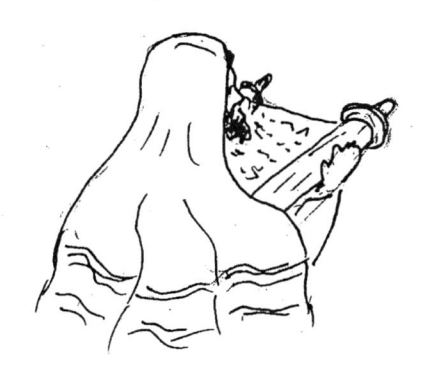

Rosh Hashanah

pronounced rush-ha-shun'-nah
Hebrew for "the head of the year"
(see the Book of Leviticus in the Bible: 23:24,25)
observed in Sept./Oct.

Rosh Hashanah is the Jewish New Year. The Bible uses a different name, Yom Truah (pronounced yome-true-ah') which means "The Feast of Trumpets." On Rosh Hashanah people gather together to hear the sound of the shofar -- the trumpet or ram's horn (see "shofar"), and to assess their spiritual condition as they approach the coming day of judgement ten days later on Yom Kippur or the Day of Atonement. (see "Yom Kippur")

Although there is a healthy sense of solemnity on this day as Jewish people reflect on their lives, it is nevertheless a very happy time as the mishpochah or extended family (see "mishpochah") gathers together for the holiday. Apple is dipped in honey to symbolize a hoped for sweetness in the year ahead. (If you want to wish your Jewish friends a Happy New Year you can say it in Hebrew: "L'shanah tovah," pronounced Luh-shun'-na-toe-vah'). I definitely remember this as a joyous time, although my family (being secular) didn't have a clue as to what it meant. We celebrated because it was TRADITION! (If you

82

haven't seen the movie, "Fiddler on the Roof", see it. It's wonderful! You'll understand tradition!)

Yom Kippur

pronounced yome-kee-poor′
or yom-kip′-per

Yom Kippur means the "Day of Atonement" in Hebrew
(see the Book of Leviticus in the Bible: 23:27-32)
observed in Sept./Oct.
(The term "High Holidays" refers to Rosh Hashanah -- see "Rosh Hashanah," and Yom Kippur together.)

Yom Kippur is the holiest and most somber day of the year, a day of national repentance and judgement. In ancient Israel it is when the High Priest entered the Holy of Holies in the Temple (the dwelling place of God's Presence) to put the blood of the sacrificial animal on the altar as atonement or covering for sin. Since there is no longer a priesthood or blood sacrifices (as the Temple was destroyed in 70 A.D.**) the commemoration of Yom Kippur is done by repentance, prayer and fasting. A final blast of the shofar (see "shofar") signals the end of the fast. It is interesting that the confession of sin is recited using the collective "we" rather than the individual "I". (For example: "Forgive us for the sins we have committed before thee...") On Yom Kippur Jews "share" each others transgressions and the general responsibility for the sins of mankind.*

* see appendix, "The Jewish Mind-set"

** see: "A short (very short) history of the Jewish people"

Sukkot or Sukkus
pronounced sue-coat' or
sook'-us
Hebrew for "booths"
Known as "The Feast of Booths" or
"The Feast of Tabernacles"
(see the Book of Leviticus in the Bible: 23:34-36)
observed in Sept./Oct.

Sukkot is a festival commemorating how God sustained the children of Israel in the wilderness after they left Egypt. The people were to live in temporary booths for 7 days and to rejoice over God's provision and His Presence. Many Jewish people still construct booths in their yards or synagogues for this holiday. The booths represent the hastily set-up dwellings the Jews used in their 40 years of wandering in the wilderness.** They are roofed with branches (the stars must be visible from the inside) and decorated with fruits and flowers. The family eats in the sukkah (the booth) and some people sleep in them. They are vivid symbols of the temporary nature of our life here on earth. Sukkot is also a harvest or thanksgiving festival, held at the time when the crops have been harvested in Israel. Sukkot is a wonderful example, along with the Passover Seder (see "Passover") of how God creates living dramas grounded in sensory experiences to make His Truth known to His people.*

* see appendix, "The Jewish Mind-set"

** see: "A short (very short) history of the Jewish people"

Hanukkah

pronounced ha'-new-kah
sometimes spelled Chanukah (the ch is a gutteral German kh -- beginning with a rattling in the back of the throat)
Hebrew for "dedication"
Hanukkah is also known as "The Feast of Dedication" or "The Feast of Lights"
observed in Nov./Dec. (usually Dec.)

Hanukkah commemorates the dedication of the Temple after it was recaptured from the evil tyrant, Antiochus, in 165 B.C. In an effort to wipe out the Jewish culture and religion, Antiochus had desecrated the Temple and forbade the Jews to practice any of their sacred rituals, such as observation of the Sabbath, or even circumcision of their children. They were commanded to build pagan altars, to sacrifice swine, and to let themselves be defiled with every kind of impurity so that they might forget the Laws of God. Whoever refused to act according to the command of the king was put to death. The Maccabees were a band of Jews who chose to oppose the evil Antiochus and arose to fight. They waged guerilla warfare for 3 years which ended in victory even though they were hopelessly outnumbered. (3,000 Jews to 47,000 Syrians!) According to tradition only a small amount of holy oil was found when the Maccabees prepared to rekindle the golden menorah or candelabra (see "menorah") and rededicate the Temple for worship. The amount of oil would last only one day, but 8 days were needed to prepare additional oil to light the remaining candles. Nevertheless, by faith they relit the menorah and it remained burning for 8 days. The conclusion was that "a great miracle happened there."

Hanukkah, then (or "the Feast of Dedication" or "The Feast of Lights") is celebrated for 8 days, during which there is the lighting of a special menorah. Each night for 8 nights a new candle is lit, until on the 8th night the whole candelabra is filled. The daily candles are lit by a 9th candle, the shammash (pronounced shah'- mahsh) or servant candle. (The traditional menorah has 7 candles.)

Hanukkah is a very happy holiday and is observed with parties, games, and gifts to the children. In western countries it is customary for a gift to be given for each of the 8 days of Hanukkah. A wonderful culinary delight, latkes, are traditionally eaten on this holiday, as are other foods made with oil (because of the miracle of the oil). See "latkes" and if possible get a hold of some or make some. Goody, goody!

89

Purim
pronounced poor'-im
in Hebrew "pur" means "lot"
also known as "The Feast of Lots"
observed in Feb./Mar.

Purim commemorates the rescue of the Jews of Persia from Haman's plot to destroy them, as told in the Book of Esther in the Bible. Lots had been cast by Haman, Minister to King Ahaseurus, to determine the date on which the Jews in Persia would be slaughtered. A miraculous deliverance occured through two Jewish people, the beautiful Queen Esther and her uncle Mordecai. Haman ended up being executed on the same gallows he had erected to kill Mordecai.

On Purim, in synagogues and temples, the Megillah (the scroll of Esther) is read. Whenever the name Haman is mentioned the children boo and jeer and spin ratchety nosemakers called groggors around and around. Gifts of food are exchanged with friends, and feasts, dances, and masquerades are held. Children especially dress up in costumes as one of the characters in the story. According to Leo Rosten, in Israel Purim is celebrated with public processions complete with floats and costumes and private masquerade parties. I guess this is the closest thing to a Jewish carnival! (but a godly one)

On a more serious note, Purim is an illustration of God's watchful care over His people and how He works through individuals (in this case, Esther and Mordecai) to accomplish His plans.

My memories of Purim are of little boys with mustaches and a delicious pastry called hamantaschen. (see "hamantaschen")

If you want to wish your Jewish friends a happy Purim, you can say "Good yontif" (yun'-tiff) which means "Good (or happy) holiday." This applies to all Jewish holidays except Yom Kippur (too solemn).

PART THREE

Jewish Foods

bagel

pronounced (as if there is anyone on this planet who doesn't know) bay'-gil Yiddish, from the German beugel:
"a round loaf of bread"

Believe it or not, according to Leo Rosten, the first mention of bagels is to be found in the Community Regulations of Cracow, Poland, for the year 1610! -- which stated that bagels would be given as a gift to any woman in childbirth. (I'm sure she appreciated it then, too!) By definition a bagel is a hard doughnut-shaped roll, simmered in hot water for 2 minutes before baking, then glazed with egg white. The traditional Jewish breakfast -- bagels lathered with cream cheese and topped with lox (smoked salmon) is not so traditional after all. It actually started in America, but whoever did start it was a culinary genius in mine humble opinion!

Cream cheese and lox can also be put on a bialy (pronounced bee-al'-lee, rhymes with dolly). The word bialy is an abbreviation of "Bialystoker" after the city of Bialystok in Poland where this wonderful thing came from. A bialy is a flat breakfast roll, shaped (in Leo Rosten's words) like a round wading pool (because it is not empty in the center like a bagel.) Sometimes it's sprinkled with onions. It kills me that I have not been able to get a real bialy since I left New York. If you've never had a bialy this won't mean anything to you, but if you've ever had one you would be very sympathetic!

<u>blintz</u> (plural, blintzes)
    pronounced blintz (rhymes with chintz)
  Yiddish, from the Russian blini: "pancake"

A blintz is a thin pancake, rolled around a filling (usually cottage cheese), sauted and served with sour cream. Blintzes today may contain any number of things besides cottage cheese, such as strawberry, cherry, or blackberry jam, apples, peaches, even potatoes. This is one of my favorite things in the whole world. I just can't get enough of them. I included the plural (blintzes) because it is impossible to eat just one.

Recipe for Blintzes

Blintz wrappers:
    4   eggs, beaten
    1   cup milk
    1   cup flour
    1   teaspoon salt

Combine beaten eggs with milk and salt. Gradually add this mixture to flour. Beat until smooth. Heat a heavy 6" skillet and grease lightly with butter. Pour in only enough batter to make a very thin pancake, tilting pan from side to side to cover bottom. Fry on one side only, until blintz blisters. Turn out onto floured waxed paper, fried side up. Repeat until all batter is used.

Cheese filling:
- 1 pound dry curd cottage cheese (this is called farmer cheese -- don't use regular cottage cheese, it's too wet)
- 2 tablespoons flour
- 2 tablespoons sugar or 1 or 2 tablespoons honey (taste for desired sweetness)
- 1 teaspoon ground cinnamon

Mix together cheese, flour, sugar or honey and cinnamon. Place a well-rounded tablespoon of mixture in center of blintz wrapper. Fold over both sides toward center and roll into envelope shape. Sauté blintzes in butter on both sides until brown. Serve with sour cream or jelly. Makes 6 servings.

borsht

    pronounced boarsht
    Yiddish, from the Russian borshch

Borsht is a beet soup served hot or cold (it's better cold), often with a dab of sour cream (Mm), sometimes with little potatoes or cucumber slices (Mm, Mm), a staple of the Jewish diet and really good too.

"The Borsht Belt" refers to an area in the Catskill Mountains of New York where there were a lot of Jewish resorts that employed entertainers (especially comedians). Many famous ones got their start here, including Mel Brooks, Milton Berle, Sid Caesar and Jerry Lewis.

Recipe for Borsht

- 9 beets, with 2-3 inches of beet tops
- 6 cups water
- 1/2 teaspoon salt
- 1 tablespoon sugar or honey
- 2 tablespoons lemon juice
- 6 small boiled potatoes
- sour cream
- sliced cucumber

Scrub beets clean, leaving tops on.

Combine beets and water in a medium saucepan and bring to a boil. Cover and simmer over low heat for about 1 hour or until beets are tender. Remove beets and slip off their skins. Pour soup into a bowl. Rinse saucepan. Slowly pour beet cooking liquid back into pan, leaving last few tablespoons soup, which may be sandy, behind in bowl; discard this liquid.

Grate beets coarsely in food processor or with grater, or you can just slice them. Return to soup and add salt and sugar. Cook 2 minutes, stirring, over low heat. Remove from heat and add lemon juice. Taste and adjust seasoning; soup should be slightly sweet and sour.

Serve hot or cold with a round tablespoon of sour cream and a boiled potato on top of each serving, or cucumber slices floating on them.

Makes 5 or 6 servings.

challah

pronounced khal´-leh (the ch is a gutteral German kh -- beginning with a rattling in the back of the throat) challah is sometimes pronounced khal´-lee (rhymes with holly)

Hebrew

Challah is a braided loaf of white bread, made with egg and glazed with egg white, traditionally made for the Sabbath (see "Sabbath"), and other Jewish holidays. There are no words to describe the ever-so-soft cake-like texture and delicate flavor of this holiday delicacy. It's not a good idea to be in the same room with challah if you are trying to lose weight.

gefilte fish
  pronounced ge-fill'-teh fish
 Yiddish, from the German for "stuffed fish"

Gefilte fish is chopped or ground fish mixed with crumbs, egg and seasoning, cooked in a broth and usually served chilled in the form of balls or oval-shaped cakes. This is traditionally served at the Sabbath dinner (see "Sabbath"). Nowadays you can buy bottled gefilte fish in a supermarket, but there are still people who remember live fish swimming around in their bathtub before the Sabbath. (I'm not one of them, thank God!)

hamantaschen
pronounced ha'-men-tosh-en
named after Haman (see below)
and the German tasch: "pocket"

Hamantaschen are triangular pockets of dough filled with poppy seed or prune jelly, eaten during the feast of Purim. (see "Purim") which celebrates the foiling of the plot of the evil Haman to destroy all the Jews in Persia. Legend has it that the triangular shape comes from the type of hat Haman wore, but this is unlikely since this style of hat was popular in 18th and 19th century Europe, not in ancient Persia, where they mostly wore round turbans. It is more probable that Jewish bakers made poppy seed pockets, which are called "muntaschen" in Yiddish, and as a play on words renamed them hamantaschen.

Recipe for Hamantaschen

Dough:
- 3/4 cup vegetable oil
- 1 cup sugar
- 3 eggs
- 1/2 cup liquid from prunes (see prune filling below)
- 4 3/4 cups flour
- 2 teaspoons baking powder
- 1/2 teaspoon salt

In a large bowl mix together oil, sugar, eggs and liquid from the prunes until well-blended. Sift together and add to this mixture. Blend dough together well and refrigerate, covered, for at least 1 hour.

Remove dough from refrigerator. Divide dough into 3 parts. Roll each piece out to 1/4" thick on well-floured board. Cut out 3" rounds. Put 1/2 tablespoon filling on each round. Fold 3 sides up to the center and pinch edges together to shape a 3-cornered hat with a hole in the middle to show the filling. Bake on a greased baking sheet, slightly apart, at 375° about 12 minutes, or until golden brown.

Prune filling:
- 12 ounces pitted prunes
- 2 lemons, sliced
- boiling water to cover prunes
- 1/2 cup walnuts, finely chopped
- 1 apple, peeled and finely chopped
- 1/4 cup honey or 1/2 cup sugar
- 1 teaspoon cinnamon

Cover prunes and lemon with boiling water. Let stand 1/2 hour or bring to a boil and simmer 10 minutes. Drain juice and reserve. Put all filling ingredients in food processor and process until well-mixed.

Knish
   pronounced Kni-ish′
  Yiddish, from Russian or Ukranian

A knish is a little dumpling filled with buckwheat groats or potatoes -- also sometimes other things are included like broccoli or spinach, etc. A good knish is something to die for but alas! I have not had a good one since I left New York. Knishes make a great nosh (see "nosh"). Little tiny ones are served with toothpicks sticking out of them at Jewish weddings.

Kreplach

pronounced krep'-lach (the ch is a gutteral German kh -- beginning with a rattling in the back of the throat)
from the German "kreppel"

Kreplach are triangular or square dumplings that contain chopped meat or cheese, etc. usually served in soup. I think you get the idea that kreplach are Jewish ravioli.

Recipe for Kreplach

Dough:
- 1 egg, slightly beaten
- 1/4 teaspoon salt
- 1 cup flour, sifted

Filling:
- 2 tablespoons onion, minced
- 2 tablespoons butter
- 1 egg
- 1 cup cooked ground beef
- 1/2 teaspoon salt

Make dough by beating ingredients together with wooden spoon. Knead on floured board until elastic. Roll paper-thin; cut into 2"-3" squares. Mix ingredients for filling; place heaping teaspoon on half of each square. Fold remaining half over top to make triangles. Press edges together securely. Drop into large pot of boiling salted water, cover tightly and cook for 20 minutes. Makes 6 servings.

Kugel
pronounced Koog'-el (pronounce the "oo" as in "good")

German

Kugel is a noodle pudding and is it good too! Kugel is traditionally made for the Sabbath (see "Sabbath") because it can be prepared beforehand and kept warm in the oven. (One is not supposed to work on the Sabbath, which includes cooking or even lighting a fire.) Most every Jewish woman can whip up a kugel (even me!) and there are many variations. It is extremely easy to make and extremely delicious. Try it, you'll like it.

Recipe for Kugel

- 1/2 pound broad egg noodles
- 3 eggs, beaten
- 1 pound cottage cheese
- 4 tablespoons sour cream
- 1/4 pound butter
- 1/2 cup raisins
- 1 teaspoon salt
- 1/4 cup sugar or honey (around 1/8 cup)
- 1 teaspoon cinnamon

Prepare noodles according to package directions; drain well. Mix together in bowl with remaining ingredients. Place in greased 11"x 7" baking dish. Bake for 1 hour at 350° or until golden brown. Serve with additional sour cream if desired. Makes 6 servings.

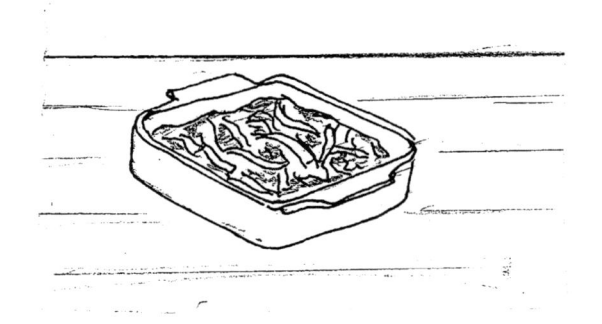

Latkes
pronounced lot'-kehs (rhymes with vodkas)
Russian for pancakes

Latkes are potato pancakes, traditionally served at Hanukkah (see "Hanukkah"), with either sour cream or apple sauce. What can I say about these superb little beauties! I don't normally eat fried food but for latkes I make an exception. Grab hold of one of your Jewish friends at Hanukkah and beg her to make you a batch. You'll be hooked forever.

Recipe for Latkes

- 6 potatoes, raw, medium size
- 1 medium onion
- 3/4 cup matzoh meal (or flour)
- 2 eggs
- 1/2 teaspoon salt
- 1/4 teaspoon pepper

Grate potatoes and drain well in colander. Add grated onion, matzoh meal or flour, eggs, salt and pepper. Drop by large tablespoons onto hot, greased griddle or frying pan. Cook until crusty brown; turn and repeat on other side. Makes 1 dozen.
Serve with sour cream or applesauce.
(You can use a food processor or blender.)

matzo (or matza)
  pronounced mott'-seh
   (rhymes with lotsa)
   Hebrew

Matzo is a brittle, flat piece of unleavened bread eaten during Passover (see "Passover") to commemorate the the Jews' exodus or flight from Egypt when they made bread without leaven because they did not have time to wait for the dough to rise. I love to have matzo with lots of butter and salt.

Matzo balls are small dumplings made with matzo meal. They are usually found floating around in matzo ball soup, traditionally eaten on the Sabbath. (see "Sabbath").

I just had to include a recipe for chicken soup which is followed by a recipe for matzo balls (which are also found in chicken soup).

Recipe for Chicken Soup

  5   pounds chicken parts
       (backs, necks, etc.)
3 1/4 quarts water
  2   onions, peeled and halved
  2   cloves garlic, peeled and halved

1 1/4 tablespoons salt
3 carrots, peeled and sliced
  several sprigs parsley
1 teaspoon dried dillweed

Place first four ingredients in a large pot (at least 5 quarts). Bring to a boil, skimming off fat as it rises to top. Lower heat, cover pot and simmer for 2 hours. Add carrots, salt and parsley; simmer 1 hour more. Stir in dillweed; heat for 15 minutes and serve. Makes 12 cups of soup.

Note: This is even better if refrigerated overnight before serving. The hardened fat can be removed before re-heating. This soup can also be strained into a clean pot and served with sliced carrots and small bits of the chicken.

Recipe for Matzo Balls

6 eggs, separated
1 teaspoon salt
1/8 teaspoon pepper
2 tablespoons melted chicken fat or vegetable oil
1 cup matzo meal

Beat egg whites until stiff. Beat egg yolks separately until light. Add salt, pepper and melted fat to yolks; fold gently into egg whites. Fold in matzo meal 1 spoonful at a time. Refrigerate for at least 1 hour. Moisten hands and form batter into walnut-sized balls. Drop into large pot of rapidly boiling chicken soup or water. Reduce heat and cook slowly, covered, for 30 minutes. Makes 12 servings.

And how could I leave out a recipe for chopped liver, that most famous of all Jewish appetizers, and from whence comes the saying, "So what am I, chopped liver?" meaning, "Do I count for nothing?"

Recipe for Chopped Liver

1 pound chicken livers, washed and drained
3 medium onions, chopped
1 clove garlic, mashed
1/4 cup oil

2 hard-cooked eggs
1 teaspoon salt
　pepper

Dry the chicken livers with paper towels. Sauté the onions and mashed garlic in oil until brown. Remove from pan and add chicken livers. Cook until they have lost their red color. Turn heat down to medium and simmer for 10 minutes. Remove from heat. Put all ingredients in food processor or blender in batches. Blend until mixture resembles a fine paste. Correct seasoning, if necessary. Serve in small scoops on lettuce leaves as a first course or as a spread for matzo. Serves at least 12 as a spread, or 6 as a first course.

PART FOUR

The Language of Judaism and Jewish Tradition

A Short (very short) History of the Jewish People

Just so that you will know what I mean when I make reference to some aspect of historical Judaism in this section, here is a brief (very brief!) synopsis of the history of the Jewish people:

@ 2100 B.C. — God calls Abraham to be the Father of the Jewish race. He leaves his home in Ur (in what is now modern Iraq) and goes to Canaan (modern Israel). This is the era of the patriarchs -- Abraham, Isaac and Jacob.

@ 1800 B.C. — The Israelites (Jews) end up in Egypt to escape a famine. They thrive for a long time but then are enslaved by a nasty Pharoah. (The incredible story of Joseph comes in here. It is too long to recount but you can read about it in the Book of Genesis in the Bible, chapters 37-50.)

1446 B.C. — Moses leads the Jews out of Egypt by way of the Red Sea (it parts and lets them across, then the water comes back again to drown all of

Pharoah's pursuing troops.) The Ten Commandments are given to Moses by God on Mt. Sinai, along with the Torah, the first 5 books of the Hebrew Bible. (see "Torah")

1406 B.C. After 40 years of wandering in the wilderness the Jews enter Canaan once again. The Jewish people worship God in the Tabernacle, a portable tent sanctuary erected and re-erected over and over as the Jews move from place to place.

959 B.C. The Jewish King Solomon (son of King David) builds the First Temple in Jerusalem to worship God. In the Temple there was a priesthood and daily sacrifices of animals as an atonement for the sins of the people.

930 B.C. The Kingdom of Israel is divided into two -- the Northern Kingdom consisting of 10 tribes, subsequently referred to as the "10 lost tribes" (although they now seem to be reemerging in different parts of the world), and the Southern Kingdom, consisting of the tribes of Judah and Benjamin.

722 B.C.	The Northern Kingdom is taken into captivity by Assyria (an ancient Empire in what is now parts of modern Turkey, Iraq, and Iran).
586 B.C.	The Southern Kingdom falls and the Israelites are taken into captivity to Babylon (modern Iraq). The First Temple is destroyed by the Babylonians.
516 B.C.	The Jews remain in Babylon for 70 years. After Babylon is captured by Persia, a Persian King allows them to return to Israel where they rebuild the Temple in Jerusalem.
70 A.D.	The Second Temple is destroyed, this time by the Romans, and the Jewish people are scattered throughout the world. This is known as the Diaspora or The Exile.
May 14, 1948	The nation of Israel is established and the Jewish people begin returning to their Promised Land. (see "Israel")

The 3 Branches of Judaism: Orthodox, Conservative and Reform

Orthodox Jews adhere most strictly to the Torah (see "Torah") as interpreted in the Talmud -- the rabbinical or Oral Law. (see "Talmud")

The Conservative branch of Judaism holds a modified view of the sanctity of the Torah and is flexible in its submission to the authority of the rabbinical law.

Reform Judaism does not require strict observance of either the Torah or rabbinical law.

I think you get the idea that each branch is a little -- and sometimes a lot -- less strictly observant of either the Torah or the Talmud.

As far as how many Jewish people are followers of each branch, most Jews who practice their religion are Reform Jews and somewhat less are Conservative. Orthodox Jews are a definite minority.

Ashkenazim and Sephardim

Ashkenazim is pronounced
osh-keh-noz'-zeem
Ashkenaz means "Germany" in Hebrew
Sephardim is pronounced seh-far'-deem
Sephardi is Hebrew for "Spanish"

Ashkenazim and Sephardim are the two main groups of people with a Jewish heritage. The Ashkenazim come from central and eastern Europe -- Germany, Austria, Poland, Hungary, etc.; the Sephardim from Spain and Portugal.

Ashkenazic Jews are distinguished from Sephardic Jews in the language they spoke, their style of thought, their culture and many aspects of their liturgy.

Ashkenazic Jews spoke Yiddish and were generally the peasants who followed orthodox tradition and scorned the secular world and secular knowledge. The vast majority of Jews in the United States are descendents of the Ashkenazim.

Sephardim were the intellectual sophisticates, well versed in secular knowledge, who rose to positions of great prominence as physicians, financiers, philosophers, mathematicians, and advisors to kings -- in Spain, Portugal and North Africa. Sephardim spoke Ladino (a form of Spanish with Hebrew elements) as opposed to Yiddish, and their writers wrote mostly in Arabic! There are only about 500,000 Sephardim and about 13-15 million Ashkenazim, although many of the Sephardim who were expelled from Spain in the 15th century (some say 1 out of 5 Spaniards!) and who ended up in South America, are discovering their Jewish ancestry and heritage. There are estimated to be between 20-25 million (!!) of these Sephardic Jews.

As for style of thought and culture, you are holding in your hand a perfect example of Ashkenazic-ness, or "Yiddishkeit." I have no idea what the Sephardic style of thought is. I can't even imagine a Jewish person not knowing any Yiddish! But I know there are Ethiopian Jews (the Falashas) and Oriental Jews, and Jews of practically every other nationality, (most of whom have never even seen a bagel -- an unsettling thought).

The Ancient Jewish Wedding

In ancient tradition the father of the groom selected a bride for his son. A betrothal period followed which was so much stronger than our modern idea of engagement that couples would need to get a divorce in order to annul the contract! During the one year betrothal period the groom prepared the home for his bride. The exact time of the groom's arrival was to be a surprise, and the bridal party would therefore be anxiously waiting, even keeping their oil lamps burning til late in the evening, just in case the wedding was to begin. Finally, at the sound of the shofar (see "shofar") the groom would lead a procession of lighted torches and musicians through the streets of the village to the house of the bride where he would "carry" her back to his house. The high point of this joyful celebration was the marriage supper that went on for a full 7 days of food, music and dance.

Orthodox Jews still celebrate a wedding for 7 days running and even among the non-Orthodox or non-observant Jews many customs unique to Judaism are practiced, such as the chuppa (see "chuppa") and the breaking of the glass (see "mazel tov"). And need I say anything about food, music and dancing!

Adonai
pronounced ah-doe-noy´
Hebrew for "Lord" or "My Lord"

Adonai is the sacred title of God. The only time it is pronounced by Orthodox Jews is during solemn prayer with the head covered. At all other times when God is mentioned Orthodox Jews say "HaShem," meaning "The Name."

The 4 Hebrew letters, YHVH, form the Hebrew name for God. Adonai is used as a substitute for these sacred letters. We do not know how YHVH was pronounced in ancient times, as there are no vowel letters in the Hebrew Torah scrolls. (see "Torah") In English YHVH is pronounced "Yahweh" or "Jehovah." Only in the ancient Temple in Jerusalem was YHVH permitted to be spoken.

Bar Mitzvah

    pronounced bar-mitz'-vah
In Hebrew bar means "son"
and mitzvah means "commandment"
therefore Bar Mitzvah means
   "son of the commandment"

The Bar Mitzvah is a ceremony held in a synagogue or temple in which a 13-year old Jewish boy assumes the religious and ethical duties of a man. After years of study and preparation the Bar Mitzvah (as the boy is called) actually leads a part of the synagogue service by saying various prayers in Hebrew and chanting the traditional weekly reading from the Torah (see "Torah") and the Prophets in the Bible. Then he gives a little speech or mini-sermon in which he thanks family and friends for participating in this joyous occasion. A celebration follows, with food and dancing and the giving of gifts which usually includes the father giving his son a tallit (see "tallit") or prayer shawl of his own.

The Bar Mitzvah ceremony obviously is very meaningful and touching and there is a lot of kvelling (see "Kvell") by parents and grandparents. Nowadays Bar Mitzvahs can be very elaborate, huge catered affairs complete with a chopped liver statue of the Bar Mitzvah boy (unlikely, but you understand what I mean.)

In recent years some congregations have introduced a Bat or Bas Mitzvah ceremony for girls, the equivalent of the Bar Mitzvah for boys. (Bat or bas means "daughter" in Hebrew, therefore Bat Mitzvah means "daughter of the covenant.") This is held when the girl reaches the age of 12 (since girls mature earlier than boys).

If you have the good fortune to go to a Bar or Bat Mitzvah be prepared to say mazel tov! (see "mazel tov!") and do Israeli folk dancing. (It's very easy. You'll love it!)

bris or brit
pronounced briss or britt
brit means "covenant" in Hebrew
the "brit milah" refers to the circumcision ceremony

The brit milah or bris (as it is called by most American Jews) is the ceremony of circumcision performed on the 8th day of a boy's life. This is sometimes done by a mohel (pronounced moy'el) who is not a rabbi but an expert in this particular area (ouch!), or by an M.D. Chapter 17 in the Book of Genesis in the Bible records that God confirmed His covenant with the Jewish people by providing "a sign of the covenant" -- circumcision on the 8th day.* A rather elaborate ceremony has developed within traditional Judaism to observe this custom such as passing the baby from one person to another, each of whom fulfills a different symbolic role. This is followed by a celebration and proclamations of "mazel tov!" (see "mazel tov!")

Amazingly enough, the blood clotting factor in an infant's body is not fully developed until the 8th day of life. Nowadays babies are circumcised on the 2nd day in hospitals after they are given a drug to approximate this factor. This doesn't sound kosher to me. (see "kosher")

127

* A covenant is a binding agreement between two parties. A covenant differs from a contract. A contract is based on mistrust (in that it is a guarantee against someone going back on his word). It has a definite time period after which it is no longer in effect. A covenant is based on mutual trust, a pact made unto death -- irrevocable (not able to be retracted or revoked). The covenant between God and the people of Israel is the Bible itself, in which God promises to bless, protect and guide the Jewish people, and they in turn promise to live a virtuous life and obey and teach God's Law. As Leo Rosten puts it, circumcision actually imprints into a man's body a sign that Israel will be perpetuated through him and that his seed, passing through the place of circumcision, will create children who will be pledged to the Jews.

broche
pronounced braw'—kheh (the ch is a gutteral German kh—beginning with a rattling in the back of the throat)

A broche is a blessing or a prayer of thanksgiving and praise to God. Almost all Jewish prayers start with a blessing to God: "Blessed art Thou..." For example, before eating food one says, "Blessed art Thou, O Lord our God, King of the Universe, who bringest forth bread from the earth." (When I went to summer camp this was said before every meal—in Hebrew and then in English.) Sometimes broches were said in the synagogue, while others were part of daily life. In the second century a famous Jewish rabbi said that every Jew should recite a hundred blessings daily. (That means about one every 10 waking minutes!) Blessings were said for almost everything: upon arising, upon drinking or eating at any time, after a safe journey or deliverance from danger, upon recovering from an illness, upon seeing a beautiful person or animal, upon seeing a natural phenomenon such as a rainbow, or lightning, or a beautiful sunset, upon putting on a new garment, smelling a fragrant odor, upon the arrival of a new season, etc., etc., etc.! This sounds to me like a life-style of thanksgiving and praise to God!

cantor or chazzen

cantor is pronounced cant'-or
chazzen is pronounced khozz'n (the ch is a gutteral German Kh -- beginning with a rattling in the back of the throat)
In Hebrew chazzen means "a seer"

The cantor or chazzen is the trained professional singer who leads the worship service in a synagogue. The cantor is a virtuoso, singing long passages of liturgy. He sings out the opening words of a prayer which the congregation takes up. Although the melodies are not written down they are standardized, so that anyone entering a synagogue can know from the cantor's melodic line whether it is an ordinary service, a Sabbath, Passover or Rosh Hashanah. (see "Sabbath", "Passover" and "Rosh Hashanah") Many times the music is very mournful because the cantor "speaks" for the congregation in experiencing all the emotions of the Hebrew text, such as suffering, compassion, contrition, etc., and of course, gratitude to God.

Cantors generally have very big voices and their singing is very flowery with a lot of falsesetto. I'm not an opera fan, but cantors always remind me of Mario Lanza. (I know, I'm dating myself.)

Chasidim

pronounced khah-seed'-em (the ch is a gutteral German kh--beginning with a rattling in the back of the throat)
sometimes spelled "Hassidim"
Hebrew for "pious," "pious ones"

The Chasidim are members of a sect of Jewish mystics founded in Poland about 1750 in opposition to the formalized Judaism of the period. Israel ben Eliezer, its founder (also known as the Baal Shem Tov, "Master of the Divine Name") preached a simple folk gospel that was full of joyous worship and spontaneous personal happy prayer. The Chasidim danced and clapped hands while singing praise to the Lord and according to Leo Rosten "invited group expressions of religious rapture."

The Chasidim still live in small communities in New York, Chicago and Boston. I remember passing their neighborhood when I was growing up in Brooklyn, where they stood out in their black coats and their custom of wearing payess (pay'-ess), long uncut ear-ringlet hair. (Orthodox Jews also dress this way, but not all Orthodox Jews are Chasidic.) Leo Rosten says that in the section of Brooklyn where they live, the main street is sometimes called Rue de La Payess. Modern Chasidim are not as joyous as those in the original sect. (I think things changed when the founder died.)

chuppa

pronounced khu'-peh (the ch is a gutteral German kh -- beginning with a rattling in the back of the throat)

Hebrew for "chamber" or "covering"

The chuppa is the wedding canopy used in most all Jewish weddings. It is usually made of embroidered white silk or satin and sometimes it is a traditional prayer shawl or tallit (see "tallit"). The canopy can either be free standing or with 4 hand-held poles, the male relatives of the couple holding each one of the poles at the corners. In American synagogues the chuppa is often a canopy of greens and flowers.

From ancient times the chuppa has been a symbol of a new household. It used to be that the bride left her father's house to go to her new husband's house -- which was symbolized by the chuppa. (see "The Jewish Wedding") I was not married under a chuppa and my husband did not break the glass with his foot (see "mazel tov") and to this day I only feel 99.99% married. (Don't tell my husband this.)

<u>daven</u>
   pronounced dah!-ven
       Yiddish, origin unknown

To daven is to pray while swaying back and forth and moving the head up and down in a rocking motion. This is the way most Orthodox Jews pray. It seems to be a way of engaging the whole body, as well as the soul, in the act of communing with God. If you ever see pictures of Orthodox Jewish men praying at the Wailing Wall you will see them davening. (The Wailing Wall is a wall in the old city of Jerusalem believed to be a remnant of the Second Temple and revered by Jews as a place of pilgrimage and prayer.)

Israel
Eretz Yisroel
Zion

Eretz Yisroel is pronounced
eh'-retz yis-roe-ail'
Hebrew for "the land of Israel"

Zion is a synonym for the land of Israel and sometimes refers to Jerusalem pronounced tzee'-yone in Hebrew

Eretz Yisroel, the land of Israel, has been the focus of the hopes and dreams of the Jewish people, "The Promised Land," since the destruction of the Second Temple in 70 A.D. and the scattering of the Jews throughout the world. ** Finally and miraculously, on May 14, 1948, the nation of Israel was born in a single day, as the Bible prophesied over 2700 years ago! (In the Book of Isaiah 66:8). Even the Jews' ancient national language, Hebrew, was restored as the Bible said it would be: "For I [God] will restore to the people a pure language..." (Zephaniah 3:9). Hebrew is called a "pure" language in the Bible because there are no words of vulgarity or profanity in Biblical Hebrew!

The Bible also predicts the miraculous

victories that Israel would have over her enemies. During the 4 major wars that Israel fought she was outnumbered 5 to 1 in soldiers, 3 to 1 in enemy aircraft and tanks, 8 to 1 in artillary, and 18 to 1 in missiles, and yet she won against these incredible odds. Over and over again Israel's small population of several million Jews defended themselves successfully against a population of what was at that time approximately 140 million Arabs!

When the Jews returned to Israel they found dry, parched, barren deserts, and an agricultural transformation began to occur. The Bible says, "the desert shall ... blossom as the rose." (Isaiah 35:1) The tiny nation of Israel is number three in the world for exporting cut flowers, the most important of which are roses! Every sort of fruit and vegetable is grown there as well, so that not only does Israel produce enough food for its own citizens, but it exports 20% of its total agricultural product to other countries. So much for a dry, parched, barren desert!

God also prophesied through the prophet Amos in the Bible that "they shall build the waste cities and inhabit them..." (Amos 9:14) What were once "waste cities" are now modern metropolis' such as Jerusalem, Tel Aviv, Haifa and many others. Israel has also excelled in technology, universities, the sciences, defense, medicine, and numerous other areas. Israel is exactly what the Bible predicts it would be. It is a modern miracle! *

* For this information about Israel I am indebted to Sid Roth's book, "They Thought for Themselves," specifically the chapter, "The Amazing Jewish Book," written by Manny Brotman. (see bibliography)

** see: "A short (very short) history of the Jewish people"

menorah
pronounced men-awe'-ra
Hebrew for "candelabra"

The menorah is the 7-branched candelabra that was lit in those places where the Jews worshipped God -- first in the Tabernacle (the portable sanctuary) when the children of Israel wandered in the wilderness for 40 years and then in the Temple.* In the Bible God gives specific instructions to Moses detailing the design of the menorah. Originally, of course, it was an oil lamp until candles replaced oil lamps in the 18th century.

The menorah represents the bringing of God's light to the world and has come to symbolize the Jewish people and the nation of Israel. The Bible says it was to be made of one piece of pure gold, an expression of purity and oneness, both of God and His people.

The menorah most people are familiar with is the special 9-branched candelabra lit during Hanukkah (see "Hanukkah").

*see: "A short (very short) history of the Jewish people"

mezuzah
pronounced meh-zooz'-ah
in Hebrew mezuzah means "doorpost"

A mezuzah is a small oblong container that is affixed to the doorframe of a Jewish house as a sign that a Jewish family lives within. Inside the mezuzah is a tiny rolled-up piece of paper or parchment on which are printed verses from the Book of Deuteronomy in the Bible: 6:4-9 and 11:13-21. The first sentence is Israel's great watchword that proclaims the Jews' faith, the Shema (pronounced sheh-ma'): "Hear, O Israel, the Lord our God, the Lord is One." The rest of the verses speak about loving God and diligently keeping His commandments. (see "Shema Yisrael" for a discussion of these verses) One of them contains the injunction to write these words "upon the doorposts of thine house."

The mezuzah consecrates the home, which is so very important in Jewish life. (To consecrate is to set something apart as sacred or holy.) In fact, the Jewish home is a temple.* It is customary to kiss the fingers and touch the mezuzah as one enters the house to show one's love for God and His word.

* see appendix, "The Jewish Life-Style"

mikvah
pronounced mick'-va
Hebrew for "a pool of water"

The mikvah is a ritual bath for the cleansing of impurity to make one ceremonially clean -- that is, able to participate in sacred rituals (such as the duties the priests carried out in the Temple). (The mikvah is not meant for physical cleansing, just spiritual cleansing, as people must bathe before they enter it.) In the first century King Solomon had constructed 2,000 "baths" for the priesthood in the Temple and no one could enter the Temple precincts without first immersing in a mikvah. Since the destruction of the Temple in 70 A.D. the custom of mikvah changed. However, modern Judaism retained the mikvah in some situations, such as the cleansing of a woman after her menstrual period and for the immersion of Gentiles who wish to convert to Judaism. Orthodox men will also immerse in the mikvah before the Sabbath or one of the Holy Days. *

In Bible times the mikvah was a stone enclosure in which the water had to be "living water", that is, it had to link to a natural running water supply like a stream or spring or contain rain water. Both men and women practised immersion regularly. Today the practice of mikvah is followed only by Orthodox Jews (the most strictly traditional).

An interesting note: Under rabbinical law, a husband and wife could not come into close physical contact, much less have sexual relations, during her menstrual period and for 7 days afterward until she immersed in a mikvah on the 7th day. Oy, vey! (see "oy!")

* There is a Biblical principle in the Mosaic Law (the Laws of God Moses recorded in the Bible) that any contact with death brings ritual impurity. Therefore coming into contact with bodily fluids such as semen or menstrual blood (signifying death in the sense that a possible conception has not taken place) will make one ritually unclean, that is, unable to take part in sacred ceremonies until cleansing in a mikvah. After the healing of certain diseases such as leprosy there is also the need for immersion, since disease is a brush with death. One also becomes ritually unclean after contact with certain unclean animals and any vessels they touched, and if one has participated in idol worship.

minyon
pronounced min'-yon
Hebrew for "number" or "counting"

Minyon is the term for the 10 Jewish males required for religious services. No prayers can begin until there is a minyon. To have 10 males is to have a synagogue or a congregation.

I never experienced this myself, but I read that if you travel by EL AL (the Israeli airline) or in an Israeli train, you often see a group of Orthodox men gathering at the back of the plane or carriage at the time of prayer. If they don't have the required number, one of them goes around tapping likely looking travellers on the shoulder to persuade them to join and make up the minyon.

<u>rabbi</u>
   pronounced rabb'-i (rhymes with dab-i)
   from the Hebrew rabi (pronounced rab-bee')
   meaning "my teacher"

A rabbi is an ordained spiritual leader of a Jewish congregation. Ordination, however, did not become institutionalized until modern times. Leo Rosten notes that the first rabbis were not clergymen at all, but men superior in character and learning whom the community respected. They exercised moral leadership and acted as judges and counselors. Even as late as the 19th century rabbis were not expected to preach sermons. They were too busy studying, teaching, and interpreting the Law. Today, of course, rabbis do pretty much what a minister does. (For a discussion of the original function of rabbis see appendix, "The Jewish Life-Style.")

shalom
pronounced sha-lohm'
from the Hebrew root word meaning "whole," "entire;" shalom means "peace"

Shalom is a word which has no equivalent in English, or any other language that I know of. We translate it to mean "peace" but it is really much more than that. It means "wholeness" or "completeness," "total well-being," lacking nothing in body, mind and spirit -- resulting in peace, health, safety, soundness, prosperity, rest and harmony. This is what God promises to His people in the Bible -- a covenant* of shalom. You can't get any better than that!

In Israel, shalom is used both as a greeting, meaning "hello," and a farewell, meaning "good-bye." Sometimes Israelis say "shalom aleichem" (pronounced a-lay'-khem, the ch that guttural kh), which means "peace unto you."

God promises in the Book of Isaiah in the Bible that if we trust Him and keep our minds stayed (focused) on Him, He will keep us in perfect peace (shalom).

* see "bris" for the meaning of "covenant."

Shekhinah

pronounced sha-khee´-neh (the ch is a gutteral German kh -- beginning with a rattling in the back of the throat) Hebrew for "Divine Presence," literally "dwelling"

The Shekhinah is the actual, radiant shining Presence of God Himself. The Shekhinah appeared to Moses in the burning bush (as recorded in the Book of Exodus in the Bible, chapter 3), and to the children of Israel as a cloud by day and a pillar of fire by night. (Exodus 13:21) There are many other instances in the Bible of the appearance of the Shekhinah. According to Leo Rosten, observing Jews believe that the Shekhinah descends on each Jewish home during the Sabbath. (see "Sabbath")

Shema Yisrael

    pronounced sheh-ma' yis-roe-ail'
    meaning "Hear, O Israel"
    shema is Hebrew for "hear"
    Yisrael is Hebrew for "Israel"

Shema Yisrael is the most common of all the Hebrew prayers, a proclamation of the Jews' faith. It is recited 3 or 4 times a day by an Orthodox Jew and it is the last prayer on his lips before he dies.

It is found in the Book of Deuteronomy in the Bible, chapter 6, verses 4-9:

"Hear, O Israel: The Lord our God, the Lord is one! You shall love the Lord your God with all your heart, with all your soul, and with all your strength. And these words which I command you today shall be in your heart. You shall teach them diligently to your children, and you shall talk of them when you sit in your house, when you walk by the way, when you lie down, and when you rise up. You shall bind them as a sign on your hand, and they shall be as frontlets between your eyes. You shall write them on the doorposts of your house and on your gates."

A beautiful prayer of total surrender and consecration (being set apart) to God.

shivah

pronounced shi'-vah (rhymes with river)
from the Hebrew: "seven"

Shivah refers to the 7 days of mourning for the dead beginning immediately after the funeral. Jewish people "sit shivah" in the home of the person who died. During the shivah period the mourners remain in the house and do not work. A minyon (see "minyon") of 10 men come to the house to hold services and to recite the Kaddish or mourner's prayer. (Actually the Kaddish does not even mention death, but it is a prayer exalting God's name and affirming faith in the establishment of His Kingdom.) Other traditional practices during this period include sitting on stools or low benches, covering mirrors, and wearing garments with a rip in the lapel (symbolic of the rending of the garments, the age-old sign of grief).

The 7-day shivah period is followed by a 30-day period of lesser mourning in which the grieving continues as life slowly begins to normalize, and then an 11-month period during which the mourner recites the Kaddish daily, preferably in the synagogue. Thereafter the deceased is remembered each year on the anniversary of the day he or she died. Jews are usually buried within 24 hours of death in a simple wooden casket. Embalming is not normally permitted, nor is there an open casket.

The Jewish approach to death is both realistic and compassionate. The shivah and further mourning periods provide the mourner with a way to honor the deceased and deal appropriately with grief. This is in accordance with Solomon's words in the Bible: "to everything there is a season," "a time to weep and a time to laugh, a time to mourn and a time to dance" (Ecclesiastes 3:1, 4).

shofar
pronounced show'-far
Hebrew for "trumpet" and specifically a "ram's horn"

The shofar is a ram's horn that is blown in the synagogue during the holidays of Rosh Hashanah and Yom Kippur (see "Rosh Hashanah" and "Yom Kippur") to summon the people to repentance. The bend in the shofar represents the head that is bowed and the human heart bent in true repentance before the Lord.

The ram's horn has special meaning to the Jewish people because Abraham, offering his son Isaac in sacrifice, was reprieved when God decided that Abraham could sacrifice a ram instead. (The ram was caught in a thicket by his horns.) This is recorded in the Bible in the Book of Genesis, chapter 22.

For 40 centuries the ram's horn has been the trumpet that has called God's people to repentance and faith. In ancient times it was also used to alert the people to danger, for calling them to assembly and war, and to announce a religious fast or feast. Its piercing sound is a summons to turn from the mundane and focus on the Divine.

In actuality there are many kinds of shofaret (plural), taken from sheep, goats, antelope and gazelles. (Only the horn of a cow is forbidden because it is a reminder of the golden calf incident at Mount Sinai recorded in the Book of Exodus in the Bible, chapter 32). The very long, spiraled horn that is commonly used is the Yemenite* shofar, which is the horn of the Kodo, an African antelope. The notes that are sounded are not haphazard, but a complicated series of traditional prescribed blasts which amounts to an art form!

Everytime I hear the shofar sound I feel a stirring in my soul, a call from deep within. It is said that satan, who before his rebellion and fall was the worship leader in heaven, had every musical instrument <u>in</u> his body -- that is, his body contained all the different instruments -- except the shofar! Therefore satan flees in terror at the sound of the shofar, which some say is the voice of God.

* Many Jews come from Yemen, a country at the southern tip of the Arabian Peninsula (south of Saudi Arabia).

Star of David

The Star of David is also known as the Magen David or Mogen David -- the "Shield of David" in Yiddish. (Magen is pronounced mawl-ghen.)

The Star of David is the 6-pointed star that is the national symbol of Israel and the Jewish people.

Would you believe no one really knows its origin, but there is a lot of speculation about this. Some say that in order to honor the beloved King David, the Jews created a battle shield to identify their soldiers, made by using the Greek "delta" (an equilateral triangle), instead of the Hebrew letter "daleth" (d), because Greek was the common language of that time. They interlocked two triangles to reflect the double daleth in David's name.

The Star of David is on the Israeli flag and identifies the Jewish people and Judaism more than any other symbol.

synagogue
pronounced syn'-a-gog
Greek for "assembly" or "congregation"

The synagogue is the place where Jewish people meet for worship or religious study. It is also called a "shul" (rhymes with full).

The synagogue probably originated when the First Temple was destroyed and the Jews were taken into captivity in Babylon (modern Iraq) in the 6th century B.C. * There the Jewish exiles gathered together in homes for mutual support. This eventually evolved into the synagogue when a building was acquired as a meeting place and a center for community affairs. Later the Jews returned to Jerusalem and a new Temple was built, but this too was destroyed in 70 A.D. The rabbis who remained regrouped and the synagogue, which was already in place for communal prayer, now took over the function of the Temple. (In 70 A.D. there were some 4 or 5 hundred synagogues in Jerusalem alone.) The Temple sacrifices, the priesthood and the Lavish ceremonies could no longer take place, but prayer became the substitute for sacrifice as an atonement for sin and many of the Temple customs were transferred as much as possible to the synagogue. Soon it became an obligation for Jews to build a synagogue or shul as soon as a community contained 10 males or a minyon (see "minyon") and in time they were established throughout the known world as Judaism's most stable and beloved institution. The synagogue and the love of Torah (see "Torah") has kept Judaism alive and preserved the Jewish people even though they have been dispersed all over the world. (This dispersion of the Jews among the lands outside of Israel is known as the Diaspora (die-aspí-ora) or The Exile.) For a discussion of the special role of the synagogue and what took place there see appendix, "The Jewish Life-Style."

* see: "A short (very short) history of the Jewish people"

tallit
pronounced tahl-eat′
sometimes spelled tallis, pronounced tahl′-iss

Hebrew for "prayer shawl"

The image of Jews in worship is always that of the Jewish man wrapped in a prayer shawl, the tallit or tallis. Initially the tallit was not an extra article of clothing, as God commanded in the Bible that tassels or fringes were to be worn on the corners of the outer garment. The fringes or tzitzit in Hebrew (pronounced tsit-tsit) was to be a constant reminder of the commandments of God. In each tzitzit there was to be a single blue thread, exactly the same color as the High Priest's robe. This emphasized the fact that every man in Israel as the head of the family had the responsibility of being the priest in his home.* Over the years, instead of wearing the fringes as part of the regular garment, Jewish tradition developed the custom of the tallit, which is usually worn only for prayer, both in the home and synagogue. Most Jews pray with the tallit covering their head, a beautiful picture of being hidden away with God and enfolded by His love.

* see appendix, "The Jewish Life-Style"

Talmud
pronounced Tol'-mud
from the Hebrew lamed: "to study," or Lamade: "to teach"

The Talmud or Oral Law is a massive compilation of the debates, dialogues, conclusions, commentaries, and commentaries upon commentaries of the rabbinic scholars who interpreted the Torah (see "Torah"), the first 5 books of the Bible. Originally these teachings were called "the Oral Law" to distinguish them from the Written Law of the Torah, but they were finally codified and written down by about 200 A.D.

The Talmudic writings apply to everything under the sun, from theology and philosophy, law, ethics, ceremony and traditions, to marriage, divorce, diet, etiquette, medicine, agriculture, geography, history, etc., etc., etc.! Traditional Jews live not by Biblical law alone, but by the rabbis teachings and decisions <u>based</u> upon Biblical law -- The Talmud. Over time the Oral Law came to be as binding as the Written Law.

Leo Rosten makes the interesting observation that it was the Talmud that held together the Jewish people when they were so widely spread across Europe, North Africa and the Middle East (and then America), making them one religious and cultural commonwealth with a common language (Hebrew) and a common code of laws, ethics and morals. I would add that since the Torah is the foundation of the Talmud, the Torah is really the heart and lifeblood of the Jewish commonwealth, the synagogue being its institutional heart. (see "synagogue")

tefillin

pronounced te-fill´-in
from the Hebrew word tefilla: "prayer"

The tefillin (also known as phylacteries) are small leather boxes strapped to the forehead and the hand containing tiny parchments on which are inscribed passages from the Hebrew Scriptures. Tefillin are worn during morning prayers by Orthodox Jewish men.

The custom is taken from the injunction in the Book of Deuteronomy in the Bible 6:8 (and also Exodus 13:9): "You shall bind them [the Lord's commandments] as a sign on your hand, and they shall be as frontlets between your eyes." The Bible is not expressly clear on how this is to be done, but traditional Jews have always fulfilled these words in the custom called tefillin. They are worn as a reminder to the Jews that the commandments of God should be on their mind (forehead) and applied to their life (hand).

The process of putting on tefillin is elaborate and there are numerous rules regulating the way in which they may be made and under what conditions they are to be put on, taken off, and worn. According to Leo Rosten, a 16th century code lists 160 laws governing tefillin!

Torah
pronounced Toe'-rah
Hebrew for "teaching," "instruction"

The Torah consists of the first 5 books of the Hebrew Bible (also called the Pentateuch): Genesis, Exodus, Leviticus, Numbers, and Deuteronomy. These writings contain the Laws of God as recorded by Moses, therefore they are also known as the Mosaic Law. In the Torah God revealed His Nature and gave Israel instructions about how they were to regulate their daily lives. The highest ideal of every observant Jew was the study of Torah.*

Jewish people call their Scriptures the Tanakh, which is an acronym for 3 words: Torah (Law), Neviim (Prophets) and Ketuvim (Writings). The Ketuvim contain poetic and wisdom literature, such as Job, the Psalms and Proverbs. This 3-fold division constitutes the Hebrew Bible.

* see appendix, "The Jewish Life-Style"

yarmulke
pronounced yar'-mulk-kah
Polish for "skullcap"

The yarmulke, also known as the "Kippah" in Hebrew, is the skullcap worn by observant Jewish males as a sign of their submission to God. Originally the custom of covering the head only applied to the priests in the Temple who were required to wear turbans (the Temple was destroyed in 70 A.D), but later in history the larger Jewish community began to wear head-coverings. Most observant Jews wear yarmulkes only in the synagogue or perhaps during prayer and when studying sacred texts. Orthodox Jews wear them all the time.

I can't resist relating this: Leo Rosten tells in his book, "The Joys of Yiddish" that a cartoon in an Israeli newspaper showed the Pope, during his historic visit to Israel in 1964, with the President of Israel. The caption read: "The Pope is the one with the yarmulke."

yeshiva
pronounced yeh-shee'-va
Yiddish, from the Hebrew yeshov:
"to sit"
(students sat while studying)

A yeshiva is both a rabbinical college or seminary and a Hebrew elementary school with a curriculum that includes Jewish religion and culture and general education.

The yeshiva, meaning a Jewish seminary, grew out of the Bet Midrash, the "House of Study," the place where Jewish men came to study the Torah and the Talmud. (see "Torah" and "Talmud") The earliest one was established in ancient Israel and the yeshivas spread wherever Jews lived, from North Africa to Spain, France, Italy, England, Holland, etc., and especially in eastern Europe, where poor students were supported by the community. Many went from home to home, eating and sleeping in a different place each night. Some slept on the benches in the yeshiva. Very few of the students received a rabbinical degree. The purpose of the yeshiva was to produce Jews who would dedicate themselves to living according to the Torah and who would spend several hours a day for the rest of their lives studying the Talmud.

Yeshua
pronounced Yesh-shoo'-a
Hebrew for "salvation"

Yeshua is the Hebrew word for Jesus. I should actually say that Jesus is the English-Greek word for Yeshua. Because Jesus, or Yeshua, was Jewish through and through. He was brought up as a Jew, attended synagogue as a Jew, His early followers were Jews, and He fulfilled all the prophesies in the Hebrew Bible about the coming Jewish Messiah. If He was walking the earth today He would probably be eating bagels, blintzes and chicken soup. Yeshua never intended to start a new religion! He Himself says that He came to fulfill the Law and the Prophets.

In my own experience the prophesy in the Hebrew Bible that got me in relation to Yeshua was in the Book of Isaiah, chapter 53. Some verses from that chapter:

> "But He was wounded for our transgressions,
> He was bruised for our iniquities;
> The chastisement for our peace was upon Him,
> And by His stripes we are healed."
> (verse 5)

"He was oppressed and He was afflicted,
Yet He opened not His mouth;
He was led as a lamb to the slaughter...
(verse 7)

"... He poured out His soul unto death...
And He bore the sins of many ...
(verse 12)

I realized I didn't have to search very hard to see who Isaiah was talking about!

Some rabbis say that these verses refer to Israel (the whole of the Jewish people), but in order for someone to die for the sins of the world He would have to be sinless -- without spot or blemish, just like the sacrificial lambs in the ancient Temple who were slaughtered as an atonement for the sins of the people. But Israel certainly wasn't sinless, as none of us are.

Ironically, before I became a Messianic Believer (a Jew who believes that Yeshua is the Messiah), I was confused about my identity as a Jew -- I had trouble integrating my cultural "Jewishness" with Biblical Judaism. Was a Jew merely someone who was born of Jewish parents, or was a Jew someone who kept the Sabbath? Was celebrating a

Jewish Holy Day just tradition, or an empty ritual, or did it have some deep spiritual significance and relevance to my life? Then when I accepted Yeshua as my Jewish Messiah everything seemed to fall into place. All my questions were answered. I finally understood who I was as a Jew -- I felt grounded in the Jewish Biblical roots of my faith and I knew why things happened the way they did in history and in my own life. I felt "completed" as they say. A hard thing to explain -- you have to experience it.

Anyway, all I can say is that my life is changed. I experience the close relationship with God that I longed for ever since I was a child. I feel the love of God. Thank you, Yeshua! I love You!

Scripture quotations are from the New King James Version of the Bible.
Copyright © 1982 by Thomas Nelson, Inc.
Used by permission.

APPENDICES

The Jewish Mind-set

There are two mind-sets that operate in the Western world -- the Jewish mind-set and the mind-set that was handed down to us from the Greeks and Romans. They are very different, usually in direct opposition to each other. (A discussion of the Greek-Roman mind-set follows because one can't be fully understood without comparing it to the other.)

The Jewish mind-set is rooted in the Bible, beginning when God chose Abraham to be the father of the Jewish race and set a people apart for Himself -- to worship Him, to obey Him, and also to think like Him. Not that the Jews have always done this, but in so far as they have followed Biblical principles, that is the extent to which they have the Jewish (or Hebraic) mind-set.

If there is one word that can describe this mind-set it is "unity" or "wholeness." The Jews don't know from fragmented, compartmentalized thinking (characteristics of the Greek-Roman mind-set). To start with, there is no word in Hebrew for a soul without a body. The word "nephesh," translated "soul" is really a soul-body. To the Hebrew mind the soul and body are inextricably connected. A person is viewed as a unified being, a whole. This soul-body connection is reflected in the fact that all of the senses are engaged in worship. The Sabbath and Jewish Holy Days -- the festivals and feasts of the Lord, such as Passover, Rosh Hashanah, Sukkot, etc., all have particular sights, sounds, tastes and smells connected with them (see "Jewish Holy Days"), such as the lighting of the candles on the Sabbath and eating challah, the special braided Sabbath bread (see "challah"). The sound of the ram's horn or shofar (see "shofar"), the touching of the mezuzah before one enters the house (see "mezuzah"), putting on the tallit or prayer shawl (see "tallit"), and countless other Jewish customs also reflect this unity of the soul and body.

Secondly, every part of the created world is seen as good, designed by God with humanity's best interests at heart. The body and its functions -- eating, sex, physical pleasure in general, are accepted as a gift from the Creator. (There are no Jewish monks or nuns!)

In Jewish thought reason and emotion are both valued. Jews are generally passionate and unashamed of their feelings. And as for reason, they have a healthy awareness of its limitations as applied to the Divine and are very comfortable with paradox -- which is a seemingly contradictory statement that may nonetheless be true. (An example of paradox: God knows everything that is going to happen, but at the same time we have free will.) The Jews know that God defies rational, human explanations and that, to quote Marvin Wilson, "mystery and apparent contradictions are often signs of the Divine." Both reason and emotion must submit to God's Word, which is the absolute standard of right and wrong. One is expected to live a moral and ethical life based on the Biblical principles of love, mercy and justice.

In the Jewish mind-set there is a unity of the sacred (things pertaining to God) and the secular (things pertaining to the world). Holiness is found in the here and now, in everyday life. There is no retreating from the world to "find God." Marriage is considered a sacred institution. According to Jewish writer and philosopher Abraham Heschel, "something sacred is at stake in each event." (see "broche" for a discussion of the acknowledgement of God in the daily life of a Jew)

Unity extends to one's neighbors as well. In the Jewish heritage there is a sense of corporate responsibility and corporate personality. The entire community is seen as a living whole -- including past ancestors and future members. Jewish prayer employs the plural "we", not the singular "I," expressing the cry of the whole community. Each mishpochah (each extended family -- see "mishpochah") sees itself as part of a larger mishpochah -- the world-wide Jewish family. Synagogue membership is never figured on an individual basis, but according to the number of family units. Jews take very seriously the Biblical teaching that everyone is his brother's keeper and each one feels a sense of responsibility for his neighbor's needs. No one lives in total isolation from others.

The Jewish mind-set is essentially based on family relationships -- both our relationship to God and to our fellow man. God is not understood in terms of philosophy or abstract ideas, but is seen as a loving Father with all that implies -- care and concern, protection and guidance (in short, relationship!). The Israelites in the Bible were called the children of God.

Jewish people see everything in terms of family -- their own immediate family, the mishpochah or extended family, and the larger mishpochah, the whole Jewish family. And if you are not Jewish they "adopt" you.

(This book makes you an official adoptee!)

To see how the Jewish mind-set works itself out in daily life, see appendix, "The Jewish Life-Style."

We'll now take a look at the Greek-Roman mind-set. A very different picture.

The Greek-Roman Mind-set

If one word could describe the Greek-Roman mind-set is is "dualism:" matter is evil, spirit is good. The creates a split between the spiritual and the material, the soul and the body, reason and emotion, the sacred and the secular.

In this mind-set the body and its functions, being part of the material, are considered to be evil, and the body then is a prison for the soul. Passion and emotion are thought to be the cause of sin, as they are connected to the body, and the goal is to rise above them through a devotion to reason. Reason becomes the highest attribute of man.

Let us see where this mishegoss (see "mishegoss") leads to:

1) ascetism -- The notion that a person can obtain a higher spiritual state by denying the body through severe discipline (such as abstention from physical pleasure or anything enjoyable, dietary limitations, self-imposed silence, forfeiting possessions, social seclusion, etc.) and self-mortification (such as the practice of some monks in the Middle Ages who would whip themselves or sleep on a bed of nails, etc.)

In this mind-set physical pleasure is seen as a hindrance to spiritual growth.

2) "otherworldliness" -- This is where spirituality is seen as detachment from earthly concerns and retreating from the world is the way to "find God." There is a strict separation between the sacred (things pertaining to God) and the secular (things pertaining to the world), and life becomes compartmentalized, divided into separate categories or compartments with different rules operating in each sphere. This allows someone to be very "religious" and yet cheat his employees or lie to gain an advantage, etc.

3) The denigration of marriage -- The institution of marriage is seen as an inferior way of life because it is a concession to the physical impulses. You can guess where this leaves the family! It is well known that by the First Century the Greek-Roman family structure had totally broken down.

4) an obsession with individualism -- With the disintegration of the family unit comes a disregard for the needs or sufferings of others and a focus on one's own desires and concerns. Selfishness becomes the norm.

5) a split between the head and the heart -- When reason is elevated and passion or emotion considered inferior and something to be denied, one becomes dry, cold and unfeeling (robot-like) -- a detached passive onlooker.

6) alienation from God -- In Greek-Roman thinking there is absolutely no contact between God and creation (man). God and matter are separated, they have no relationship. God has no human qualities, in fact He is without any qualities at all. He is only understood in terms of philosophy and abstract ideas.

7) relativism -- Without any contact or communication between God and man, man cannot hear God's voice to tell him what is right and wrong, what is true and what is false. Therefore there can be no absolute Truth. Truth is relative -- it changes with different circumstances.

Some of you may be wondering how it is that there are groups within Christianity, which is based on Biblical Judaism (after all, we call it the Judeo-Christian tradition) who seem to have many of the elements associated with the Greek-Roman mind-set, such as priestly celebacy, "otherworldliness," the notion that poverty is more spiritual than prosperity, etc. The answer is that although the first Christians were Jewish (with a Jewish mind-set!), Gentiles then started entering the Church in large numbers, bringing elements of the Greek-Roman mind-set with them into the Church. Christianity became a peculiar mixture of Greek-Roman thinking and Jewish thinking (which they could not escape altogether because the Bible is such a totally Jewish document!) It is interesting that the Christian Church is now in the process of rediscovering its Jewish roots and returning to the Jewish (or Hebraic) mind-set.

It is easy to see that a lot of the Greek-Roman mind-set still permeates Western culture in general in the form of:

- alienation from God
    God and man have no relationship, He is merely an abstract concept.

- relativism
    no absolute right or wrong, truth changes with different circumstances

- the denigration of marriage and the family

— selfishness
    an obsession with individualism
    resulting in a disregard for the
    needs and sufferings of others

This can only be countered by a return to the God of the Bible, which is to say the Jewish or Hebraic mind-set.

Note: Much of this information on the two mind-sets comes from Marvin Wilson's fascinating book, "Our Father Abraham." Thank you, Marvin!

The Jewish Life-Style

The entire Jewish culture is structured around prayer, and reading and studying the Word of God. (This occurred for centuries and centuries when the majority of mankind was illiterate!)

Here I have to quote the eloquent words of Leo Rosten in his book, "The Joys of Yiddish," speaking about the Eastern European Jewish community of previous centuries:

"Study and prayer, or (better) study-prayer was the most potent mortar in Jewish life and history. It was the linchpin in a Jew's self-esteem. It lent meaning and purpose to the most difficult and desperate of existences. It illuminated life. It ennobled, inspired, redeemed. It admitted even the humblest Jew to the company of sages, prophets, scholars, saints. Virtually all of male Jewry participated in a perpetual seminar on the Torah and the Talmud. [see "Torah" and "Talmud"] Even the cobblers. Even the tailors. The drovers and diggers, farmhands and carpenters. The peddlers and beggars and shopkeepers. Most Jews past the age of six... could read and write! They were all arguers, dialecticians, amateur theologians -- albeit their poverty was great, their living precarious, their security at the mercy of local fanatics. When studying Talmud, every Jew felt elevated, a participant in an eternal dialogue on divinity, truth, the purpose and obligations of life."

pp. 39-40

The synagogue had a very special role in the life of a Jew. Most Jews spent more of their time in the synagogue than in the market-place. They began their day there, said their prayers there, and met their friends there. The doors of the synagogue never closed. Men studied and prayed night and day, both alone and in groups. Often they sang their studies, and felt transported to a higher world.

But prayer and study was not confined to the synagogues. Someone visiting the city of Warsaw during the First World War saw a lot of coaches parked at a parking place with no drivers in sight. A young Jewish boy showed him to a second floor room where all the drivers were engaged in fervent study and religious discussion. He then found out that all the professions -- the bakers, the butchers, the shoemakers, etc. all had their own rooms in the Jewish district where every free moment which could be taken off from work was given to the study of the Torah! In almost every Jewish home in Eastern Europe, even in the humblest and poorest, stood a bookcase of volumes.

In the ancient synagogue, the synagogue ruler (who was chosen from among the elders) selected the men who would take part in worship. The first of these was the prayer leader. Prayer began with a reciting of the Shema (see "Shema Yisrael") and then the Amidah (sometimes just called "The Prayer" because it is so well known and loved), 19 short blessings that extol God's glory, petition God for such things as insight and forgiveness, deliverance from oppression and sickness, and freedom from want. Then there are petitions for national well being, such as the restoration of Israel and the ingathering of her exiles, etc. The three closing benedictions thank God for His mercies and blessings. (The Shema and the Amidah are still recited today.) Then a second person read the Torah portion for the day. After that the prayer leader returned to read the passage from the Prophets. A sermon followed which was sometimes given by the prayer leader or some visitor or other person. Judaism is a religion of lay people. Even today, as in ancient times, any member of the congregation may be called upon to read or preach. A rabbi once commented to Marvin Wilson (see bibliography) that if every synagogue were to close around the world, Judaism would survive because every Jew is expected to be knowledgeable about his faith. From the beginning Israel was called to be, as the Bible says in the Book of Exodus 19:6, "a kingdom of priests."

As for rabbis, they were originally learned men whom the community looked to for moral leadership and who acted as judges and counselors. Even as late as the 19th century they were not expected to preach sermons, but were too busy studying, teaching and interpreting the Law. They too, were considered "Laypersons." The tradition was that no one should make a living from the study of the Torah, or from teaching it. This was to be purely motivated by love and a joy in and for itself. The early rabbis all had daily jobs by which they earned their keep. There were rabbis who were farmers, street sweepers, shopkeepers, etc. The famous rabbis were all workman-scholars: Hillel was a woodchopper, Shammai, a surveyor, Ishmael a tanner, Abba Hoshaiah, a launderer.

Today, even though rabbis function in a way similar to ministers, as in the ancient synagogue, any member of the congregation may read or preach and is still expected to be a "priest" unto the Lord. This is especially true in the home, which in the Jewish faith is considered to be a temple, the man being the "priest" of the home. The presence of the mezuzah on the doorpost (see "mezuzah") signals that what was a mere house has become a Jewish home, and, in effect, a temple where men and God live together in communion. (see "Sabbath" for an understanding of the centerpiece of the Jewish life-style)

In the ancient Jewish home education began in infancy. There is a Jewish saying that 'a child sucks in knowledge of the Torah at the mother's breast.' Children learned to read the Torah beginning at 5 years of age; at 10 they began a study of the Oral Law or Talmud. By the first century there was compulsory education for all Jewish boys from the age of 5 or 6. A 5 year old boy may have learned the Hebrew alphabet at home and may have been able to read and write easy words before he went to school. His first textbook was the Book of Leviticus in the Bible (one of the most difficult even for adults!)

Rabbinic tradition tells us that it was unlawful for a family to live in a place where there was no school. The school was attached to the synagogue, but classes might be held outdoors as well, the pupils sitting on the ground in a semi-circle around the teacher. The maximum number of students in a class was 25, above which the teacher was entitled to an assistant. Girls did not attend school, but because of their future role in educating their own children, they received an education at home from their father or mother. Moral and religious training were the only aim of the school. The teaching of a trade was the task of the father.

The Jewish Life-Style Today

Many of these practices, customs and traditions are still observed by modern Jews. It all depends on how secular a Jewish person or community has become. The interesting thing about this is that I grew up in an area, and within a circle of friends and acquaintances, where there was not much talk about God, and although some people attended synagogue, most did not. And yet, in spite of this, moral and ethical standards were high, there were strong family ties (and extended family ties!) and the majority of the people I knew were socially conscious and committed to helping the needy and persecuted. So even though many spiritual aspects of the Jewish life-style are no longer observed by secular Jews, the mind-set (or belief system) underlying the life-style still remains and is reflected in how Jewish people think and act. It's as if the mind-set, after centuries and centuries, is embedded in our DNA. (see appendix, "The Jewish Mind-set") Ironically, most Jewish people don't realize that their way of thinking is rooted in the Bible, many of whom have never even opened its pages!

Well-Known Jewish People

The Entertainment Industry:
(comedians, actors, directors, producers, etc.)

Mel Brooks
Carl Reiner
Milton Berle
Red Buttons
Jack Benny
Groucho Marx
The 3 Stooges
Paul Newman
Kirk Douglas
Shelly Winters
Sid Caesar
Jerry Lewis
George Burns
Jerry Seinfeld
Woody Allen
Sarah Bernhardt
Harry Houdini
Steven Spielberg
Robert Klein
Barbra Streisand
Billy Crystal
Al Jolson
Lauren Bacall
James L. Brooks

Dustin Hoffman
Danny Kaye
Norman Lear
Bette Midler
David Sarnoff
Lee Strasberg
Sophie Tucker
Eddie Cantor
Barry Levinson
Sam Levinson
Louis B. Mayer
Samuel Goldwyn
David O. Selznik
The Warner Bros.
William S. Paley
Tony Randall
William Shatner
Leonard Nimoy
Neil Sedaka
Edie Gorme

(This list could go on and on, but I'll stop here.)

Writers:

Bernard Malamud
Norman Mailer
Allan Ginsberg
Paddy Chayefsky
Clifford Odets
S.J. Perelman
Ayn Rand
Phillip Roth
Neil Simon
Arthur Miller
Franz Kafka
Anne Frank
Ben Hecht
Elie Wiesel
Herman Wouk
Leon Uris
Marcel Proust
Gertrude Stein
Martin Buber
Boris Pasternak
Emma Lazarus
Maurice Sendak
Judy Blume
Saul Bellow
Isaac Bashevis
    Singer

Musicians:

Isaac Stern
Itzak Perlman
George Gershwin
Jerome Robbins
Paul Simon
Gustav Mahler
Felix Mendelssohn
Arnold Schoenberg
Stephen Sondheim
Benny Goodman
Leonard Bernstein
Bob Dylan
Irving Berlin
Beverly Sills
Arthur Rubinstein
Jerome Kern
Aaron Copeland
Vladimir Horowitz
Buddy Rich
Jasha Heifetz

Artists:

Marc Chagall
Man Ray
Ben Shahn
Mark Rothko
Louise Nevelson
Louis Kahn (architect)

Scientists:

Albert Einstein
Neils Bohr (father of modern quantum theory)
Robert Oppenheimer (directed the development of the atomic bomb)
Edward Teller (created the theory behind the hydrogen bomb)
Carl Sagan
Paul Ehrlich (creator of the cure for syphilis)
John Von Neumann ("father of the computer")
Selman Waksman (discovered antibiotics)
Casimir Funk (discovered vitamins)
Jonas Salk (creator of a vaccine for polio)
Edwin Land (invented instant photography: the Polaroid camera)
Sigmund Freud

Statesmen and Politicians:

David Ben-Gurion
Benjamin Disraeli
Louis Brandeis
Golda Meir
Theodor Herzl
Chaim Weizman
Menachem Begin
Henry Kissinger
Yitzak Rabin
Karl Marx
Bella Abzug

Diane Feinstein
Herbert Lehman
Arthur Goldberg
Barry Goldwater
Alan Greenspan
Ed Koch
Joseph Pulitzer
Bernard Baruch
Haym Salomon (financed the American Revolution)

Other Fields:

Sandy Koufax
Mark Spitz
Howard Cosell
George Steinbrenner
Ralph Lauren
Calvin Klein
Ted Koppel
Mike Wallace
Walter Winchell
Walter Lippmann
Larry King
Rube Goldberg
Al Capp (creator of Li'l Abner comic strip)
Ben Cohen and Jerry Greenfield (founders of Ben & Jerry's Ice Cream)
Levi Strauss (invented "blue jeans")
Jerry Siegel and Joe Shuster (created "Superman" comic strip)
Bob Kane (creator of "Batman and Robin")
Stan Lee (creator of "Spiderman")
Adam Gimbel
Helena Rubinstein

When I first started to compile this list of well-known Jews I thought it would be easy, but it turns out that everybody and his mother (especially his mother) is Jewish! I left out more than I put in, but I think you get the idea that the Jewish people have contributed much to world and American culture.

BIBLIOGRAPHY

Brooks, Philip. *Extrordinary Jewish Americans*. New York: Children's Press, 1998.

Garr, John D. *Living Emblems*. Atlanta: Restoration Foundation, 2000.

Gross, David C. *English-Yiddish/Yiddish-English Dictionary*. New York: Hippocrene Books, Inc., 1995.

Kasdan, Barney. *God's Appointed Customs*. Baltimore: Lederer Messianic Publications, 1996.

Levy, Faye. *International Jewish Cookbook*. New York: Warner Books, 1991.

Ligon, Sr., William T. *Imparting the Blessing*. Brunswick, GA.: The Father's Blessing, 1989.

Peterson, Galen. *Handbook of Bible Festivals*. Cincinnati: The Standard Publishing Company, 1997.

Rosten, Leo. *The Joys of Yiddish*. New York: Pocket Books, 1968.

Roth, Sid. *They Thought for Themselves.* Brunswick, GA.: MV Press, 1996.

Shapiro, Michael. *The Jewish 100.* New York: Citadel Press, 1994.

Wilson, Marvin R. *Our Father Abraham.* Grand Rapids: Wm. B. Eerdmans Publishing Company, 1989.

Also, much information came from a wonderful television program that talks about -- and better yet, shows -- Jewish customs and traditions (with lots of footage from Israel):

Lash, Neil and Jamie. *Jewish Jewels.* Television program. Check listings. (1-800-293-7482)

All recipes from:
Moskowitz, Melissa. *The Jews For Jesus Family Cookbook.* San Francisco: Purple Pomegranate Productions, 2005.

Quote on p. 175-6 from "The Joys of Yiddish." Copyright 1968 by Leo Rosten Reprinted by permission of William Morris Agency, LLC on behalf of the Author

Printed in the United States
130071LV00001B/33/A